Representing Landscapes

What do you communicate when you draw an industrial landscape using charcoal? What about a hyper-realistic Photoshop collage method? What are the right choices to make? Are there right and wrong choices when it comes to presenting a particular environment in a particular way?

The choice of medium for visualizing an idea is something that faces all students of landscape architecture and urban design. Each medium and style option that you select will influence how your idea is seen and understood.

Responding to demand from her students, Nadia Amoroso has compiled informative and eye-catching drawings using various drawing styles and techniques to create this collection for landscape architects to follow and – more importantly – to be inspired by. More than twenty respected institutions have helped to bring together the very best of visual representation of ideas, the most powerful, expressive and successful images. Professors from these institutions provide critical and descriptive commentaries, explaining the impact of using different media to represent the same landscape.

This book is recommended for landscape architecture and urban design students from first year to thesis, and will be particularly useful for visual communications and graphics courses and design studios.

Nadia Amoroso is the Founder and Creative Director of DataAppeal™, a data-design visualization company. She also teaches design studio and visual communications at the University of Toronto. She holds and has held a number of international academic and administrative positions including Lawrence Halprin Fellow at Cornell University, the Garvan Chair Visiting Professor, and Associate Dean. She specializes in visual representation, analog and digital graphics, and architectural and landscape architectural design. She has a PhD from the Bartlett School of Architecture and degrees in Landscape Architecture and Urban Design from the University of Toronto. She is the author of *The Exposed City: Mapping the Urban Invisibles* (Routledge, 2010).

Representing Landscapes

A visual collection of landscape architectural drawings

Edited by Nadia Amoroso

Routledge
Taylor & Francis Group

LONDON AND NEW YORK

First published 2012
by Routledge
2 Park Square, Milton Park, Abingdon, Oxon OX14 4RN

Simultaneously published in the USA and Canada
by Routledge
711 Third Avenue, New York, NY 10017

Routledge is an imprint of the Taylor & Francis Group, an informa business

Every effort has been made to contact and acknowledge copyright owners,
but the editor and publisher would be pleased to have any errors or
omissions brought to their attention so that corrections may be published
at a later printing.

British Library Cataloguing in Publication Data
A catalogue record for this book is available from the British Library

Library of Congress Cataloging in Publication Data
Representing landscapes : a visual collection of landscape architectural
drawings / Nadia Amoroso.
p. cm.
Includes bibliographical references and index.
1. Landscape architectural drawing. 2. Visual communication in art. I.
Amoroso, Nadia.
SB472.47.R47 2012
712.022'2--dc23
2011023978

ISBN: 978-0-415-58956-7 (hbk)
ISBN: 978-0-415-58957-4 (pbk)
ISBN: 978-0-203-15216-4 (ebk)

Typeset in Garamond
by Fakenham Prepress Solutions, Fakenham, Nofolk NR21 8NN

Printed and bound in India by Replika Press Pvt. Ltd.

Contents

Notes on Contributors

Michelle Arab is a Lecturer at the University of Washington (USA), College of Built Environment, Department of Landscape Architecture, and is Principal of Michelle Arab Studio. She is both a registered landscape architect and artist.

Matthew Beall is a Master of Architecture candidate at the University of British Columbia, Canada. He has a strong interest in drawing and new media as they relate to the process of design and practice of architecture.

Rachel Berney is an Assistant Professor, School of Architecture at the University of Southern California, USA. She has a PhD in Landscape Architecture and Environmental Planning, University of California, Berkeley.

Inge Bobbink is an Associate Professor of Landscape Architecture at the Delft University of Technology (the Netherlands), Faculty of Architecture. She is coordinator of the LA Masters' education program and leader of the research program Dutch Lowlands. Her PhD research, entitled "The Language of the Dutch Polder Water", investigating the landscape architectonic possibilities of the new Dutch water system, is part of this program.

Jacqueline Bowring is an Associate Professor at the School of Landscape Architecture, Lincoln University, New Zealand.

Bradley Cantrell is an Associate Professor and Graduate Coordinator at the Robert Reich School of Landscape Architecture at Louisiana State University (USA), College of Art + Design. He teaches studios, visual representation and digital representation courses.

Jeff Carney is a Research Professor at the Robert Reich School of Landscape Architecture at Louisiana State University (USA), College of Art + Design.

Eva Castro is Director of Landscape Urbanism at the Architectural Association in London, UK. She is co-founder of Plasma Studio and GroundLab, based in London.

Neil Challenger is Head and Senior Lecturer at the School of Landscape Architecture at Lincoln University, New Zealand.

Holly A. Getch Clarke is an Associate Professor at the Department of Landscape Architecture, Harvard Graduate School of Design, USA.

Paul Cureton is a PhD Candidate in Landscape Architecture at Manchester Metropolitan University, UK.

Marcella Eaton is Associate Dean (Academic), Environmental Design Program Chair and Associate Professor for the Department of Landscape Architecture at the University of Manitoba, Canada. She has a PhD in Landscape Architecture.

Andrea Hansen is a Lecturer at Harvard University's Graduate School of Design (USA). She has previously taught visual representation and advanced digital mapping and modeling techniques at PennDesign, University of Pennsylvania, USA.

Walter Hood is Principal and Founder of Hood Design, a landscape architecture firm based in Oakland, California, USA. He is Professor of Landscape Architecture & Environmental Planning and Urban Design at the College of Environmental Design, University of California, Berkeley, USA.

Jeffrey Hou is an Associate Professor and Chair of the Department of Landscape Architecture, University of Washington, Seattle, USA.

Daniel Jauslin is a Researcher and Lecturer of Landscape Architecture at the Delft University of Technology (the Netherlands), Faculty of Architecture, and a Principal at Drexler Guinand Jauslin Architects (Frankfurt, Rotterdam, Zurich). His PhD research, entitled "Architecture with Landscape Methods", is part of the Architecture and Landscape program.

Sean Kelly is an Assistant Professor at the University of Guelph (Canada), School of Environmental Design and Rural Planning, Department of Landscape Architecture.

Mikyoung Kim is Chair and Professor of the Department of Landscape Architecture at Rhode Island School of Design, USA. She is an award-winning international landscape architect and artist.

Stephen Luoni is Director of the University of Arkansas (USA) Community Design Center and the Steven L. Anderson Chair in Architecture and Urban Studies. He teaches design studios and visual communications. His design and research have won numerous awards and are well published.

Lisa Mackenzie is a Lecturer in Landscape Architecture at Edinburgh College of Art, UK.

David Syn Chee Mah is a Lecturer at Harvard University's Graduate School of Design, USA. Previously he taught at Cornell University's College of Architecture, Art and Planning, and at the Landscape Urbanism program at the Architectural Association in London. He is Co-founder of asensio_mah (with Leyre Asensio Villoria), with a number of completed and active landscape and architectural projects.

Anthony Mazzeo is a Senior Instructor in the Landscape Architecture Program at the College of Architecture and Planning, University of Colorado at Denver, USA. He is also a registered landscape architect and a Principal of GroundWorks, based in Denver.

Karen M'Closkey is an Assistant Professor at the Department of Landscape Architecture,

School of Design, University of Pennsylvania, USA. She teaches studios and visual representation courses.

Marc Miller is a Lecturer in the Department of Landscape Architecture at Cornell University, USA. His interests lie in the roles of representation, visualization and modeling in the design process using both digital and analogue media formats.

Steffen Nijhuis is an Assistant Professor of Landscape Architecture at the Delft University of Technology (the Netherlands), Faculty of Architecture. His PhD research, entitled "Landscape Architecture and GIS", deals with the application of geographic information systems to landscape architectonic research and design. He is program leader of the research program Architecture and Landscape, and coordinator of MSc theory and methodology courses in landscape architecture and urban design.

Richard Perron is Acting Head and Associate Professor for the Department of Landscape Architecture at the University of Manitoba, Canada. He has a PhD in Landscape Architecture.

Alfredo Ramírez teaches in the Landscape Urbanism program at the Architectural Association, London, and is Co-founder of GroundLab.

Chris Reed is Adjunct Associate Professor of Landscape Architecture at Harvard's Graduate School of Design (USA), and Principal and Founder of Stoss Landscape Urbanism, a Boston-based strategic design, landscape architecture and planning practice. He also taught at the John H. Daniels Faculty of Architecture, Landscape, and Design at the University of Toronto, Canada, and at the University of Pennsylvania School of Design, USA.

Eduardo Rico teaches in the Landscape Urbanism program at the Architectural Association, London, and is part of GroundLab.

Daniel Roehr is an Assistant Professor at the School of Architecture and Landscape Architecture at the University of British Columbia, Canada. He organizes sketching tours abroad, most recently to Italy in 2008 and Iran in 2007, and teaches introductory and advanced media, studios and landscape engineering.

Roberto Rovira is an Associate Professor and Chair of Florida International University's Landscape Architecture Department in Miami, Florida, USA, and Principal of Azimuth Studio, Inc. He obtained an MLA from the Rhode Island School of Design in 1998, and a BS from Cornell University in 1990. He is the recipient of numerous awards that recognise his work in areas that explore the shifting relationship among cities, landscapes and ecologies.

Max Hooper Schneider holds a Master's in Landscape Architecture from Harvard Graduate School of Design, USA.

Becky Sobell is a Senior Lecturer in Landscape Architecture at Manchester Metropolitan University, UK.

Jason Sowell is an Assistant Professor for the Department of Landscape Architecture at the University of Texas at Austin (USA), School of Architecture.

Chris Speed is a Reader in Digital Spaces at Edinburgh School of Architecture and Landscape Architecture, Edinburgh College of Art, UK. His interests lie in the engagement of digital technology with the field of architecture and human geography through a variety of established international digital art contexts. He holds a doctorate from the University of Plymouth, UK.

Chip Sullivan is a Professor at the College of Environmental Design at University of California, Berkeley, USA. He is author of the well-known *Drawing the Landscape* (Wiley, 1997).

Jamie Vanucchi is a Lecturer for the Department of Landscape Architecture at Cornell University, USA. Her interests lie in ecology, design and representation.

Richard Weller is Winthrop Professor and Chair of the Landscape Architecture program for the Faculty of Architecture, Landscape and Visual Arts, University of Western Australia. Weller has over twenty-five years' experience in landscape architectural design practice, visual communication and academics.

Kongjian Yu holds a PhD in design from Harvard University's Graduate School of Design, USA. He is Dean and Professor of the Graduate School of Landscape Architecture at Peking University, China, and a Visiting Professor at the Harvard Graduate School of Design. He is President and Principal of Turenscape, a landscape and urban design firm based in China.

Foreword

Walter Hood

How do we graphically represent the environmentally dynamic, ever-changing social, cultural and political landscape? Within the two-dimensional logic of an image, how do we describe the sensorial and aesthetic qualities of landscape? These are questions that arise when any collection of landscape representations are assembled.

Within academia and practice, drawing conventions have not changed much over the years. The plan view, section, elevation, perspective and paralline drawing are a mainstay. The perspective view remains the best "picture" to describe our design intentions. Piero della Francesca's *Ideal City* conveyed the Renaissance's perfect symmetry and order; Humphrey Repton's *Red Books* utilized before-and-after perspective views extolling the social, cultural and environmental values of the time; the single-line perspective cartoons of modernism featured machine-age accoutrements that exuded pure optimism for the future; rendered drawings (Color Marker and Prismacolor) of the 1970s and 1980s flattened the landscape's legibility into a fun and happy picture; and images from the current technological context allow us to be wherever and whomever we want to be. All in all, the graphic, two-dimensional, logical picture reflects the time, values and attitudes of its authors and peers.

The graphic representations of landscape in academia today continue this tradition, defining their epoch. The sampled image drawings produced today are socially full, presenting a public in an ecologically rich landscape. In many cases, the rhetoric that accompanies these drawings advocates different ways of representing the landscape. The nomenclature no longer romanticizes landscape experience and type, but seeks to elucidate landscape performance – field conditions, mats, grounds, generative operations and transects. As a sign of our times – when "green" is a populist brand, ecological sustainability is mandated, and issues of class, race and culture cloud safety issues – landscape representation projects a proscenium full of technology, natural performance and gleeful people. Wind turbines, wetlands, woods, verdant pastures and a homogeneous public are comingled to suggest optimism for the future through the medium of pure landscape.

What is most visible and optimistic in the landscape representations selected here is drawing – the presence of the hand. A decade ago, landscape academicians worried that maybe the computer would literally render our environments, and that "drawing" would be lost. And for a moment, the graphic "poster" has stood in for representation. This collection of landscape representations from various academic programs illustrates the acculturation of technology with drawing. In many cases, they are seamlessly integrated in their logic and appearance. This publication offers a handsome collection of student drawings that depict various kinds, qualities and types of landscape, using a broad range of media and techniques. Utilizing sampled overlays, scanning and layering, the lines and marks of the authors emerge. The representations seem to search for a new graphic narrative that describes the specificity of time, place and its natural and cultural processes, while introducing a design work – a project composed of landscape.

Acknowledgments

This book would not be possible without the efforts and support of key individuals.

I would like to acknowledge all the contributors from various universities and institutions across the globe who have dedicated their time and efforts to making this publication a reality. Their ongoing collaboration, dedication to teaching, and expertise in visual representation of this subject matter have helped crystallize this visual collection into this book. Supplementary to this, of course, are the authors' assistants and teaching assistants, without whose generous efforts this book would not be possible. I had a pleasure reconnecting with colleagues and establishing new connections with international colleagues. Thanks go to: Chris Speed, Lisa Mackenzie, Becky Sobell, Paul Cureton, Eduardo Rico, Alfredo Ramírez, Eva Castro, Steffen Nijhuis, Inge Bobbink, Daniel Jauslin, Kongjian Yu, Neil Challenger, Jacqueline Bowring, Richard Weller, Marc Miller, Jamie Vanucchi, Roberto Rovira, Holly A. Getch Clarke, Max Hooper Schneider, Andrea Hansen, David Syn Chee Mah, Chris Reed, Bradley Cantrell, Jeff Carney, Mikyoung Kim, Stephen Luoni, Daniel Roehr, Matthew Beall, Chip Sullivan, Anthony Mazzeo, Sean Kelly, Marcella Eaton, Richard Perron, Karen M'Closkey, Rachel Berney, Jason Sowell, Michelle Arab, Jeffrey Hou. Their advice and expertise in this subject has framed the book a broad visual resource with fruitful commentary. I would like to acknowledge Walter Hood for his beautifully composed Foreword and for helping to set the tone of this book. His ongoing passion toward landscape architectural design and representation is clearly evident in his successful career.

I would also like to acknowledge the students whose works are featured in the book; their hard work and talent have shaped this publication as a guide for other students and professional alike. Thanks go to: Nadia D'Agnone, Robert Jackson, Stacy Day, Julie Russell, Douglas Todd, Jessica Wagner, Yi Zhou, John Vuu, Elnaz Rashidsanati, Namrata Pokhral, Yasmine Abdel Hay, Henry Anderson, Hugh Barne, Rene Rhiems, Fiona Kydd,

Torbjorn Bengtsson, Paula Gillian, Hazel Cunliffe, Jacob Helm, Tom Daggers, Paul Cureton, Wen Wen Wang, Hossein Kachabi, Alejandra Bosch, Li Zhuo, Nicola Saladino, Karishma Desai, Ioannis Tsoukalas, Mai Yoshitake, Robert Mayr, Lisa Troiano, Filippo Abrami, Marita Koch, Diego Luna Quintanilla, Minije Si, Wang Sisi, Li Chunbo, Sun Qi, Xi Xuesong, Chen Lin, Xu Liyan, Matt Durning, Matthew Tidball, James McLean, Lisa Fleming, Jonathan Turner, Esti Nagy, Julia Robinson, Julian Bolleter, Alex Fossilo, Tom Griffiths, Richard Weller, Mike Rowlands, Ian Weir, Bekk Crombie, David Zielnicki, Maria Calderon, Maria Hook, Aidan Chambliss, Stina Hellqvist, Anders Lindquist, Ulrike Simschitz, Joanna Ibarra, Kevin Banogon, Brennan Baxley, Sefora Chavarria, Devin Cejas, Carolina Jaimes, Andres Pineda, Luis Jiménez, Cecilia Hernandez, Max Hooper Schneider, Leena Cho, Alexander Arroyo, Senta Burton, Michael Easler, Kate Smaby, Irene Toselli, Patchara Wongboonsin, Yizhou Xu, Judith Rodriguez, Ilana Cohen, Sandra Herrera, Xinpeng Yu, Lisl Kotheimer, Marcus Owens, Forbes Lipschitz, Alpa Nawre, Jing Zhang, Geneva Wirth, Kelly Nelson Doran, Erik Prince, John Oliver, Will Benge, Kelly Sprinkle, Joaquin Martinez, Natalie Yates, A. Baum, M. Ellender, C. LeBeau, K. Lonon, P. May, P. McGannon, S. Miller, B. Moran, A. Ramirez, C. Thonn, Stephen Comstock, Shushmita Mizan, Sean Henderson, Prakkamakul Ponnapa, Laurencia Strauss, Filomena Riganti, Eduardo Terranova, Damian Augsberger, Bo Young Seo, Graham Patterson, Eric Dempsey, Courtney Gunderson, Kelly Spearman, Lee Stewart, Christopher Sullivan, Lori Yazwinski, Cory Amos, Joshua Clemence, Jimmy Coldiron, Benjamin Curtin, Andrew Darling, Elsa Pandozi, Brian Poepsel, Michela Sgalambro, Lauren Vogl, Tim Schmidt, Peter Bednar, John McWilliams, Jody Verser, Bart Kline, Matthew Hoffman, Daniel Kuehn, Jia Cheng, James Johnson, Sheena Soon, David Guenter, Hendrick Guliker, Sara Kasaei, Matthew Beall, Ariel Mieling, Lucie Lee, Justine Holtzman, Alex Harker Cecil Howell, Iris Chang, Mari Carson, Lindsay Cutler, Kelly Smith, Erin Devine, Doug Kay, Joe Kuk, Yang Huang, Brian Caccio, Jan Jurgensen, Audric Montuno, Eryn Buzza, Stephen Heller, Matt Williams, Yang Huang, Daniel Irving, Jaclyn Marsh, Yoshi Yabe, Justin Neufeld, Tracy Liao, Shawn Stankewich, Meaghan Hunter, Kristen Struthers, Judith Cheung, Kaleigh Lysenko, Sarry Klein, Leah Rampton, Meaghan Pauls, Aiden Stothers, Tiffany Marston, Alejandro Vazquez, Francisco Allard, Joe Kubik, Gary Garcia, Meng Yang, Gabe Mason, Larkin Owens, Noah Halbach, Yvonne Ellis, Brooks Rosenberg, Sandi Veras, Cami Culbertson, Lindsey Gadbois, Matt Knorr, Win Leerasanthanah, Lisa Reynolds, Justin Martin, Matthew Martenson, David Minnery, Karen May, Peggy Pei-Chi Chi, Han Liu, Justin Miron, Jessie Gresley-Jones, Stephanie Cheng, Ana Espinosa, Liu Xin, Jeffrey Cock, Shadi Edarehchi Gilani, Zahra Awang. (Due to the lengthy list of names, I apologize if your name is missed.)

Thank you to my own students from the John H. Daniels Faculty of Architecture, Landscape and Design. It has been a pleasure advising such talented and forward-thinking individuals.

Thank you to a number of my colleagues who have been great mentors for this book: Fran Beatty, John Crone, Ina Elias, Peter Trowbridge, Jane Wolff, Maurice Nelischer, Rob Wright, Lisa Rochon and Jim Patterson. I am grateful to my past students throughout the years and across various institutions, who have inspired me to craft such a publication, and constantly allowed me to update my visual palette. They are the present and the future – thank you for your vision and support.

I would like to express special gratitude to my former students Leila Fazel and Nadia D'Agnone, for their assistance with the publication; their time and efforts are much appreciated.

Thank you to Routledge (Taylor & Francis Group) and for the editorial vision of Alex Hollingsworth, Louise Fox and their team in sharing this idea and making this publication a reality.

Finally, I am grateful to my family for their ongoing support and encouragement; and to my husband, Haim, for your devotion and patience, which has made this process a rewarding experience. To Siena, Giuliano, Sofia and Serena.

Nadia Amoroso

1 Introduction
The visual collection

Nadia Amoroso

Landscape architecture has undergone numerous shifts in modes of representation over the past several decades, and it is the responsibility of instructors in the field to assist their students in reaching their full potential, so that in the future landscape architecture will continue to grow at both aesthetic and practical levels. Upon graduating with a degree in Landscape Architecture and Urban Design from the University of Toronto, I began teaching at college level. This was a period when digital representation was the foremost standard of communication in the field, and yet it was important to maintain the influence of traditional representation methods. This presented many challenges in creating a harmonious marriage between digital and traditional methods, and in encouraging students to become excited about a range of drawing styles and techniques so as to deliver optimal drawings that would best attract audiences to their work. As a young professor teaching studios and visual representation, I was able to relate to students' struggles in depicting landscapes. As an undergraduate and graduate student, browsing through magazines such as *Topos* and *LOTUS* was the primary way to discover the latest effective modes of drawing the landscape and applying visual styles to one's work. However, while my students had the advantage of newer technologies and tools, there existed no comprehensive guide to the modes of representation that would best aid students of landscape architecture. It became one of my goals to connect these students with the most current modes available of representing cities and landscapes. Landscape journals and magazines such as *Topos*, *Journal of Landscape Architecture* (*JoLA*), *Landscape Architecture Magazine* and *Garten+Landschaft* were invaluable resources for information on the latest competitions and ways of representing landscape expressively.

My experience teaching landscape architecture at several universities and institutes demonstrated the desperate need for a readily accessible collection of visual representation styles capturing various landscape characters and types. Student feedback underscored the demand for a resource that used concrete examples of appropriate drawing styles and media to demonstrate the variety of possibilities available for landscape architecture projects. This inspired me to compile a simple visual resource comprised of successful, eye-catching drawings created by landscape architecture students. Because *Representing Landscapes: A visual collection of landscape architectural drawings* is, in part, created by students, it will serve to teach and inspire current and future students to follow in their predecessors' footsteps. Although images make up a large component of this work, they are supported by texts from professors of visual communications, graphics (both digital and hand-drawing), and studios' courses. Many of the selections were personally chosen by these instructors to illustrate the effectiveness of successful student work.

Over twenty accredited international landscape architecture programs have participated in the creation of *Representing Landscapes*. Current professors in the field, who teach design studios, visual representation and/or digital visual communication, or similar types of course, provide critical and descriptive commentaries on these images, stating clearly what styles and media are useful for expressing particular landscape types. To take just one example, the visual effect of capturing an industrial landscape in charcoal is contrasted against the aesthetic impact of a hyper-realistic Photoshop collage. The collection showcases a variety of landscape types (large parks, post-industrial sites, ecological sites, brownfields, urban plazas, woodlots, waterfronts, landscape urbanism, urban design, etc.) and characters (the image and identity of the site); and a range of media (charcoal, graphite, digital rendering, etc.) and techniques (hand-sketching with digital collage/montage, layering of multiple processes, diagramming using Illustrator, etc.) that render these landscape qualities.

The following visual essay provides an introduction to the type and quality of images presented in this publication. These images are drawn from the work of my former students at various universities.

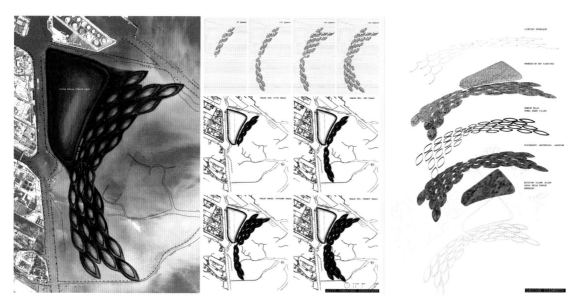

1.1 a–c

(a) Large-scale plan of an industrial site, design of formal expression rendered using charcoal with hints of shade and shadow. Charcoal rendered plan collaged onto black-and-white aerial site photo. (b) Phasing plan with small sections generated using AutoCAD and stylized using color and various pen widths in Illustrator. (c) Exploded axonometric of concept depicting systems and components of the design, rendered in AutoCAD and edited in Illustrator and Photoshop). By Nadia D'Agnone, University of Toronto.

1.2

Perspective drawing of industrial site of a concrete plant, rendered in charcoal using tone and shade to beautifully capture the essence of the space. By Robert Jackson, University of Arkansas.

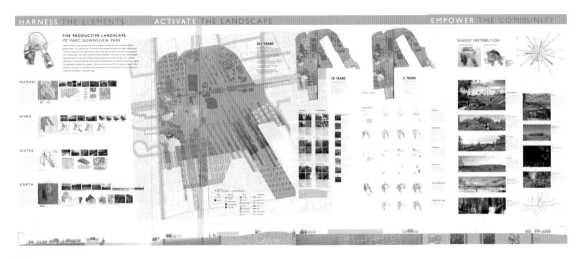

1.3

Overall site design of a large park (Downsview Park, Canada). Four large panels over 24 × 36'', joined together as a single, flowing drawing. Contains site analysis, large-scale overall concept plan, phasing plan, section at bottom of panel connecting all boards, eye-catching perspectives composed using Photoshop collage methods. Diagrams composed using Illustrator and edited in Photoshop. By Stacy Day, Cornell University.

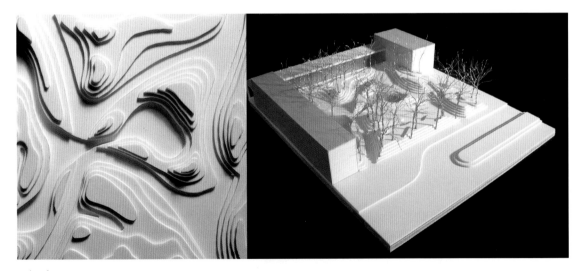

1.4 a–b

Contour model made of thin, flexible form board, later re-created to scale, used as final analogue model with steel trees and content using wood. By Julie Russell, University of Arkansas.

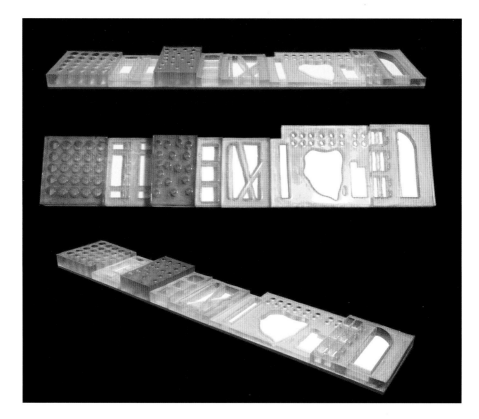

1.5

Spatial model of an urban park, made of colored resin cast from cardboard and wood base mound. Depicts the overall volumetric and spatial outcome of an existing urban park. By Douglas Todd, University of Toronto.

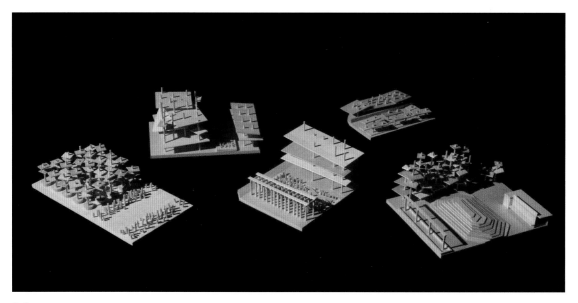

1.6

Spatial model of an urban park, delicately composed using basswood. Built as separate units of the park, which could be puzzled together as one overall park spatial system. Each section depicts the overall volume and form of the park. By Jessica Wagner, University of Toronto.

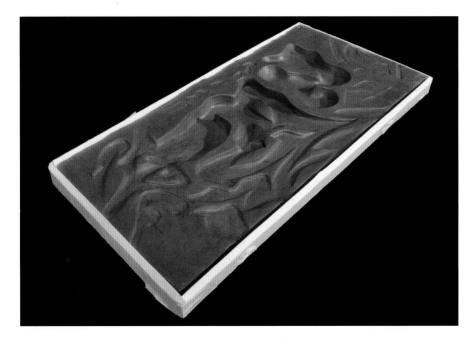

1.7
Clay model of an urban park. Surface sculptured using knife and hands, smooth finished depicting the sculptural surface quality of the site. Set-up wood frame box. By Yi Zhou, University of Toronto.

1.8 a–d
Digital model of surface form generated using Rhinoceros, followed by texture and material application. The digital form was fabricated using computer numerical control machinery. Images depict stages of output development from digital generation to 3D physical output. By John Vuu, University of Toronto.

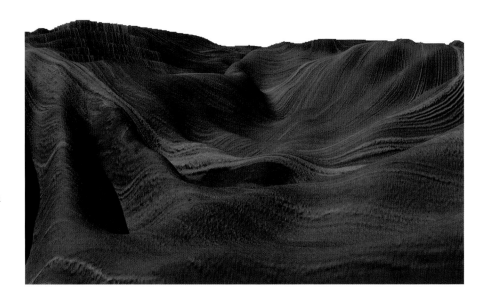

1.9
Digital landscape form with an application of sand texture, depicting a canyon. Composed using 3ds Max with V-Ray lighting technique. By Elnaz Rashidsanati, University of Toronto.

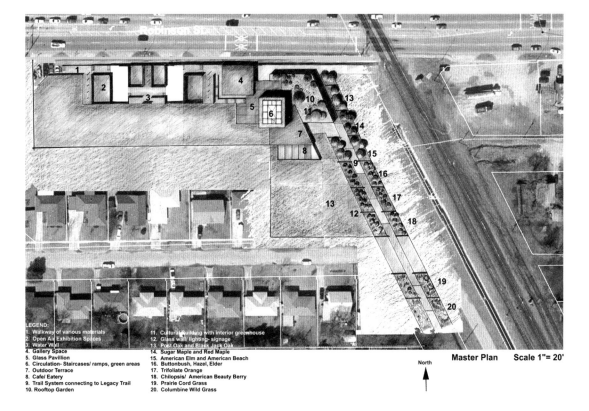

LEGEND:
1. Walkway of various materials
2. Open Air Exhibition Spaces
3. Water Wall
4. Gallery Space
5. Glass Pavillion
6. Circulation- Staircases/ ramps, green areas
7. Outdoor Terrace
8. Cafe/ Eatery
9. Trail System connecting to Legacy Trail
10. Rooftop Garden
11. Cultural Building with interior greenhouse
12. Glass wall/ lighting- signage
13. Post Oak and Black Jack Oak
14. Sugar Maple and Red Maple
15. American Elm and American Beach
16. Buttonbush, Hazel, Elder
17. Trifoliate Orange
18. Chilopsis/ American Beauty Berry
19. Prairie Cord Grass
20. Columbine Wild Grass

North

Master Plan   Scale 1"= 20'

1.10
Proposed masterplan, colored pencil plan collaged onto black-and-white aerial photo (of existing content). By Namrata Pokhral, University of Oklahoma.

1.11
Perspective. Beautifully composed image montage of a market site. Rays of light across the overall images capture the sun-saturated market space and the feel of the area. Elements of vegetation, people and textures are carefully blended and collaged into the scene using Photoshop. By Yasmine Abdel Hay, University of Toronto.

2 Representations of Space

Chris Speed and Lisa Mackenzie

Students at the Edinburgh School of Architecture and Landscape Architecture, Edinburgh College of Art are encouraged to convey a sense of atmosphere and seasonality in their work. Design proposals are communicated through a range of drawings, but of particular relevance to landscape architecture is the challenge of capturing scale within less defined contextual limits. In the external environment, the human relationship with space demands a unique, although not unrelated, architectural interpretation of thresholds and both horizontal and vertical space, particularly in relation to eye level and movement. The positioning of "actors" within the visualisations is a critical device representing the aspirations of the student in terms of how users will ultimately negotiate and experience the spaces they propose.

Students are encouraged to consider how their "drawings" operate as representations of space – but also how they offer the viewer insight into spaces of representation. The former may provide knowledge about the qualities of the environment, including aspects of its ecological, social and economic conditions. The latter give the viewer a further cultural insight into the designers' aspirations for the place, perhaps less real and more imagined, but valuable in understanding a vision for its future.

2.1 a
Rendered plan superimposed onto black and white aerial. AutoCAD, Adobe Photoshop and hand-drawn. By Henry Anderson.

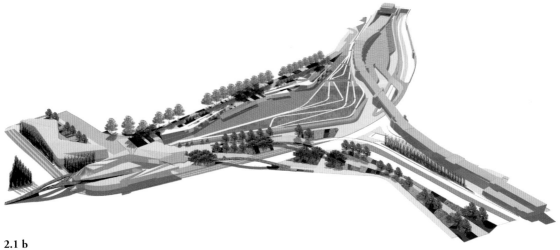

2.1 b
Axonometric view, rendered using AutoCAD, Adobe Photoshop and hand-drawn. By Henry Anderson.

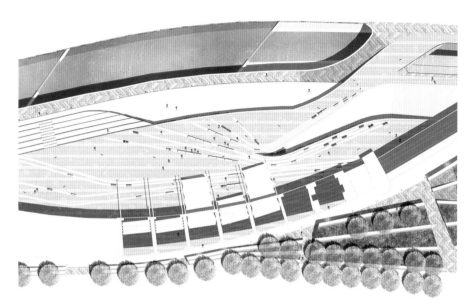

2.2 a
Design for Murano
Park. AutoCAD,
Adobe Photoshop
and hand-drawn. By
Hugh Barne.

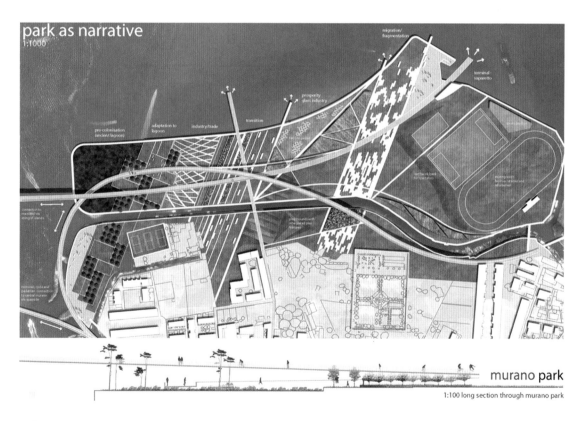

2.2 b
Design for Murano Park. AutoCAD, Adobe Photoshop and hand-drawn. By Hugh Barne.

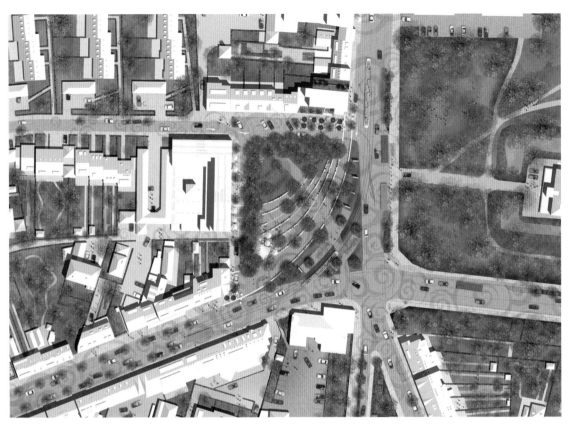

2.3
Masterplan for Bockumer Platz, Germany, drawn in CAD before being rendered in Photoshop. By Rene Rhiems.

2.4 a
Perspective/image montage using Adobe Photoshop with glow layer. By Fiona Kydd.

2.4 b
Perspective/image montage of a lagoon using Adobe Photoshop. By Fiona Kydd.

2.4 c
Perspective/image montage of urban meadows, using a combination of Google SketchUp and Adobe Photoshop with found images. By Fiona Kydd.

2.5 a
Perspective/image montage of New Canal, using Adobe Photoshop. by Torbjorn Bengtsson.

2.5 b
Perspective/image montage of an island, using Adobe Photoshop. by Torbjorn Bengtsson.

2.6
Perspective/image montage of South Street Seaport, using Adobe Photoshop. By Paula Gillian.

3 Thinking Drawing
Image typologies for processes in landscape architecture

Becky Sobell and Paul Cureton

The pedagogical approach to drawing at Manchester Metropolitan University is to encourage experimentation and openness to using drawing within landscape architecture. A re-evaluation of what makes a "good" drawing is often necessary to allow students to see drawing as a process: a tool to develop an awareness of the landscape, its effects on the people who use it, and the possibilities for future change.

The reflection contained within students' drawings is also a reflection for the tutors themselves: "To teach is to make an assumption about what and how the students learn; therefore, to teach well implies learning about students' learning."[1]

We have selected analytical and developmental student drawings to represent this approach. We see drawing as a journey – a journey for the student within a landscape, immersed in all its aspects, tactile qualities, movement and sensory environment, that is reduced to a graphic procedure. The drawing is reflective on the original process of understanding the space in which one is situated. Thus a "good" drawing may move the student through to vision and developed solutions.

One may respond to these drawings as relics of a re-evaluative activity, an artefact of an action. The process of drawing often makes explicit our unconscious notions, what John Berger describes as "burrowing in the dark, a burrowing under the apparent."[2] The student can show, through drawing, that rather than being engaged in an act of non-looking, they have really perceived the landscape. In drawing, we make real the human experience.

These processes materialize in activities such as contour drawing, a practice that formalizes looking. At the time of making, the resulting image becomes secondary to the act of drawing. Later, a re-evaluation of the drawing may bring students an awareness of their own processes of selection and editing. We encourage students to look at the landscape, and equally at their drawings of the landscape. An exploration of the immediacy of line has descriptive possibilities for the complex multiple rhythms of landscape. Drawing helps the student speak of this experience in another voice. Just like writing, it can help reflect on the nature of the site, and if, as Tim Ingold states, "[it is to be] understood in its original sense as a practice of inscription, there cannot be any hard and fast distinction between drawing and writing".[3] It is a language and vocabulary to be developed, delimited and communicated.

Drawing pedagogy must extend the idea of drawing as a "synaesthetic and communitive medium [which] might better afford a richer realization of ideas within the built environment".[4] An abstract drawing may be the most effective means of synthesizing the totality of personal experiences of one place at one time. Equally, when developing concepts into designs, the transformative nature and immediacy of drawing turn the intangible idea into tangible representations. The journey drawing takes moves through what Henri Lefebvre calls "the shadows and the light, between the conceived (abstraction) and the perceived (the readable/visible). Between the real and the unreal."[5]

In field observation, by measuring and recording space using paces as units, the student at once evaluates spaces using abstract mathematical concepts and drawing. The movement and scale of one's body is documented in the marks one makes. These marks represent a "modality of vision supported by other senses and conditioned perceptions".[6] It is reflective of place, space, movement, marks, and understanding of the landscape type one is in. By making marks, "our vision is continually active, continually moving, continually holding things in a circle around itself, constituting what is present to us as we are".[7]

An appropriate choice of medium and of drawing typology depends upon the intended function of the drawing. The function, in turn, is defined by the stage the student has reached in their project. Any landscape type may be successfully represented by any means. However, an accomplished landscape architect is able to choose from a wide visual vocabulary, and to use the resulting representation to inform the next phase of their work. As Mark Treib summarizes, "the image begins to tell us more than we have projected into it; new or unrecognized relationships or ideas emerge that stimulate creativity. Perhaps for this very reason the drawing has remained the primary vehicle for conceptualization in architectural and landscape design."[8]

Notes

1   Ramsden, P. *Learning to Teach in Higher Education*, 2nd edn. London/New York: Routledge, 1992, p. 6.

2   Berger, J. *Berger on Drawing*. Aghabullogue, Co. Cork, Ireland: Occasional Press, 2005, p. 77.

3   Ingold, T. *Lines: A Brief History*. London/New York: Routledge, 2007, p. 3.

4   Corner, J. "Representation and landscape: drawing and making in the landscape medium." *Word and Image* 8(3), 1992, p. 275.

5   Lefebvre, H. *The Production of Space*, trans. Donald Nicholson-Smith. Oxford: Blackwell, 1991, p. 390.

6   Clarke, H.G. "Land scopic regimes: exploring perspectival representations beyond the 'pictorial' project." *Landscape Journal*, 24(1), 2005, p. 52.

7   Berger, J. *Ways of Seeing*. London: Penguin, 1972, p. 9.

8   Treib, M., ed. *Drawing/Thinking: Confronting an Electronic Age*. London/New York: Routledge, 2008, p. 15.

barriers

3.1
Pen-and-pencil sketch of a rural setting. By Hazel Cunliffe.

3.2
Felt and pen spatial analysis. The use of carefully rendered tone articulates the linear movement inherent in this urban streetscape. The direction of mark-making adds a new layer of information to the illustration. By Jacob Helm.

3.3

Mixed-media collage design development/visualization. Layering and colouring over a modified photograph is used to evaluate and communicate design proposals for an under-used urban site. The selected media bring the proposed interventions to the fore, while allowing the viewer an overview of the context. By Tom Daggers.

3.4 a–b
Pencil and gouache concept visualization. A perspective for development of a former slate mine waste tip into a wetland and oak forest using water-catchers. The drawing makes use of marks in the landscape made by miners, and uses these pre-cut surface patterns to develop the form of this slow conversion. By Paul Cureton.

3.5
Pencil, thinking drawing. Graphite tonal work helps convey the "blurring of boundaries" between landscape and architecture, and the current push for uncovering the sensual, tactile qualities of the landscape and weather itself. By Paul Cureton.

3.6
Pencil, thinking drawing. Graphite tonal work helps convey the shape, topography and form of the landscape. By Paul Cureton.

4 Projective Readings
Indexes and diagrams in landscape urbanism

Eduardo Rico, Alfredo Ramírez and Eva Castro

Landscape urbanism

As part of an emergent body of work that claims landscape as a lens through which to read the city,[1] the Landscape Urbanism course in the Architectural Association (AALU) sets up an agenda of expanding existing techniques to represent the processual and systemic nature of the metropolitan environment, turning them into projective tools and ultimately opening up new definitions of what designing our cities might mean.

AALU projects draw their principles from sources such as the Boston Emerald Necklace, where city-wide storm-water-management systems are central in the provision of a coordinated network of parks within the city; or the Bronx River Parkway, where the road infrastructure is carefully coordinated with the adjacent urban fabric, catering for drivers' and inhabitants' needs. However, due to the rate of growth in contemporary metropolises, the potential of these historical examples needs to be critically revised, as the landscaping strategies linked to more picturesque traditions may not cope with the size, geometrical and functional constraints of megalomaniac infrastructure projects, fuelled by a problem-solving attitude of planners and transport engineers.

The MA Landscape Urbanism places performance of territorial elements at the core of students' design thesis, whether these are larger-scale infrastructural systems, agriculture or other productive landscapes. The fundamental difference from other disciplinary approaches is that AALU tries to use these performative elements not so much with the sole aim of providing with goods or satisfying the needs of those living far away, but as material for the exploration of spatial configurations that grasp new levels of engagement with emerging fabrics of the metropolis.

This compromise with the research of new materials for the city is what defines the approach of AALU with regard to performance and functionality, departing from an emerging trend of using optimization, energy-saving and other well-proven environmental technologies as a way of depicting developments as sustainable or defending self-referential, formally complex compositions.

Thus AALU engages with both indexing and diagramming techniques – on the one hand as they constitute the medium from which to bridge from abstract thoughts and design intentions to concrete production and proposals; and on the other as they are an operative tool to tackle the problems of homogenization in urban fabrics and the lack of responsiveness within contemporary accelerated urbanism.

Within this, the focus of the MA Landscape Urbanism on large-scale projects offers students the opportunity for a multi-scalar approach and the perfect test-bed for these tools, where traditionally territorial readings have been used to understand and clarify different aspects of the territory while limiting movement across the scales.

Indexing

As part of a preoccupation with incorporating rich territorial dynamics into the urban, Landscape Urbanism commences the work by generating a rich base of indexes, which translate environmental and socioeconomic parameters into a substrate ready to serve a more propositional approach to the use of graphic material.

In this sense, Landscape Urbanism borrows the logic already set up in McHargian[2] practices, where landscape ecology and drawing principles of relationships between parts of the territory are used to structure the proposal. The main difference resides in the use of graphic material and selection of processes to map, as the projects tend to move from fundamental constraint drawing that delimits boundaries or no-go areas into a more propositional engagement with the context. This is possible due to an attention to multiple variables beyond the ecological or, strictly speaking, environmental.

The expansion of the scope of readings prompts AALU into an approach where systematic reading of process becomes linked to a shift from delimitation techniques (in drawing terms, dead geometry) to a search for structuring patterns emerging from relevance at tectonic levels and instrumentality for planning and decision-making processes.

From here, indexing techniques enhance traditional territorial readings beyond the solely analytical or explanatory tools of the site, boosting them to translate environmental, topographical and geographical parameters into more propositional and explorative mechanisms through the use of the index:

> Index: a sign that is linked to its object by an actual connection or real relation (irrespectively of interpretation), for instance, by a reaction, so as to compel attention, in a definite place and time. A simple example is an "Exit" sign which has an arrow pointing towards the exit. Smoke billowing from a house is an index for a fire inside.
>
> Charles Sanders Peirce, 1901[3]

An index is thus understood as a construct/an alchemy/an amalgam among the territory's existent parts, which, rather than prioritizing one over the other, facilitates their interaction, and further manipulation of the system by which they are held together and ultimately operating as a whole. This leads to the generation of strategies that have at their core the affection of relationships instead of a remedial approach to the discrete parts.

The transit from the index toward the hyper-index is maintained as a continuum or zone of action that allows both to (infra)structure the ground as a means for spatial organization and to return for feedbacks and readjustments. Hence natural systems (rivers, green corridors, water channel systems), urban flows (pedestrians, vehicular), exchange of goods and products, networks of local interactions, and existing urban patterns are used to establish new frameworks from where nodes, axes, routes or paths are accentuated, enhanced or weakened; while others become spines to connect, separate or differentiate existing and new developments. This methodology leads us not towards a blank canvas completely free for experimentation, but to one that is full of information with which to work, negotiate and experiment. The purpose is to acknowledge the presence of an existent materiality within the territory and to propose modes of relating to it.

Multi-scalarity

Linked to the idea of using indexing techniques as a way of engaging with territorial complexities, there is an ambition to work with relationships between processes that happen at different scales. The indexing tools become the medium where other logics will emerge, proliferate or anchor, providing the conceptual infrastructure for a proposal that allows a multiplicity of entities to organize effects from the bottom up.

This leads to consideration of the term "scale" as a locus of exploration and research. If we read the environment as defined by the interaction of processes mediated by human actions, we can begin to speculate about what is generated by their intersection. Along these lines, scale is defined as the framework where the domains pertaining to diverse machinic processes intersect and show their co-gradiance – it is therefore an emergent property, as opposed to a graphic ratio or bounded spatial assemblage defined at the outset of a project's commission.

The skill of the Landscape Urbanist resides in identifying this potential inherent in the indexical work, and switching the nature of the work into the realm of the proposition across the scales identified. It is at this moment when the diagrammatic potential behind the drawings takes pre-eminence and guides graphic production from the reading of the existing into a projective realm of a process-defined proposal.

It is ultimately in the space between index and diagram where projects, starting from a processual and systemic reading of the environment, move to claim full responsibility for a spatial proposition across scales. The research now focuses on discovering how this *modus operandi*, inbuilt in the Landscape Urbanism code, serves as a catalyst for contemporary modes of practice and describing a way in which all professions that deal with the city may be reconfigured.

Notes

1   Waldheim, C. "Landscape Urbanism," in *The Landscape Urbanism Reader*. New York: Princeton Architectural Press, 2006, p. 15.
2   McHarg, I. *Design with Nature*. New York: Doubleday/Natural History Press, 1971.
3   Peirce, C.S. "The Commens Dictionary of Peirce's Terms". www.helsinki.fi/science/commens/dictionary.html.

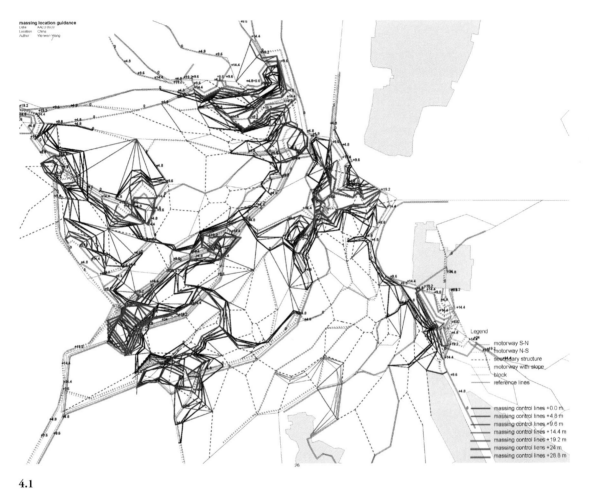

4.1

Massing location strategy for the Yangtze River Delta, China. Digital image generated in Rhinoceros and edited in Adobe Illustrator. By Wen Wen Wang.

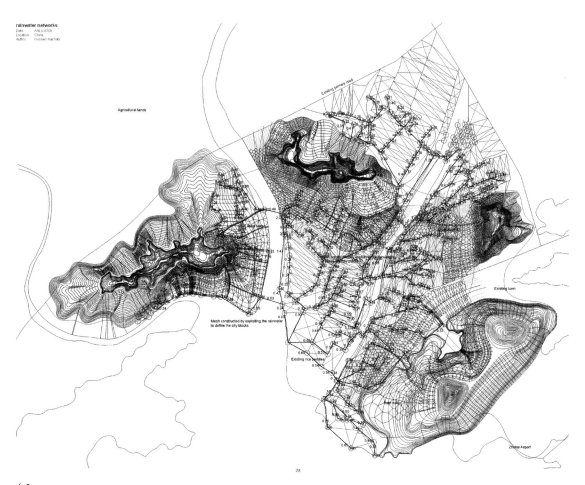

4.2
Overall strategy for Pearl River Delta, China. Digital image produced in Rhinoceros. By Hossein Kachabi.

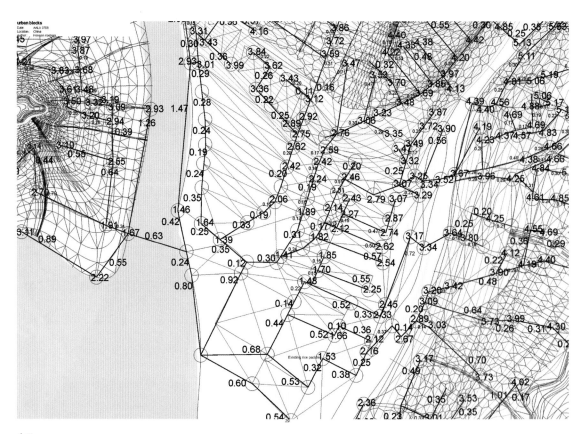

4.3
Mesh based on water structure for Pearl River Delta, China. Digital image produced in Rhinoceros. By Hossein Kachabi.

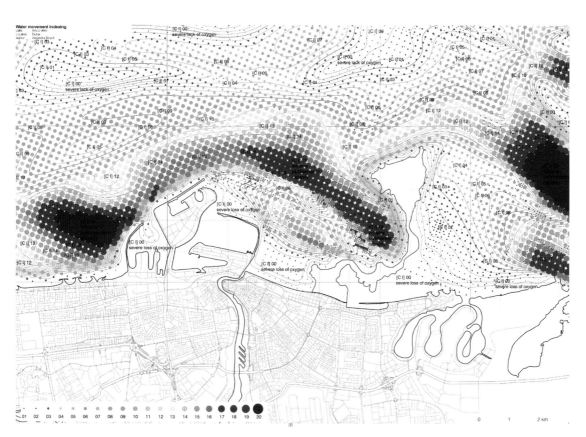

4.4
Indexing current movement and speed, Dubai. Simulation generated in Maya Autodesk and edited in Adobe Illustrator.
By Alejandra Bosch.

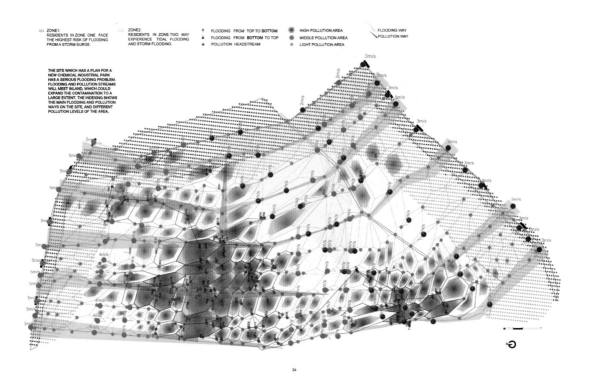

4.5
Water pollution index, Yangtze River Delta, China. Digital image produced in Rhinoceros and edited in Adobe Illustrator. By Li Zhuo.

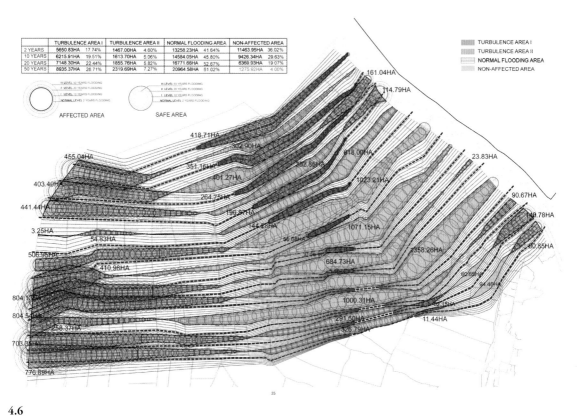

4.6
Flooding and water velocity index on canals, Yangtze River Delta, China. Digital image produced in Rhinoceros and
Grasshopper plug-in, edited in Adobe Illustrator. By Li Zhuo.

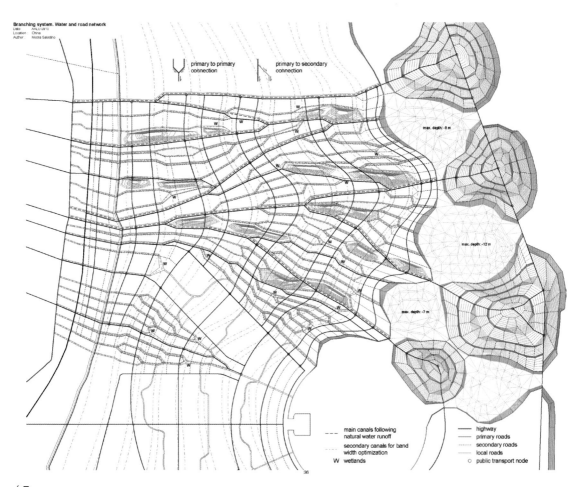

4.7
Branching system proposal for water canals for Yangtze River Delta, China. Digital image produced in Rhinoceros and edited in Adobe Illustrator. By Nicola Saladino.

4.8
Indexing proximity to infrastructures for Yangtze River Delta, China. Digital image produced in Rhinoceros and edited in Adobe Illustrator. By Karishma Desai.

5 Landscape as an Architectural Composition

Steffen Nijhuis, Inge Bobbink and
Daniel Jauslin

The specific focus of landscape architecture at the Faculty of Architecture, Delft University of Technology in the Netherlands is on understanding the formative elements behind the (urban) landscape, and on the development of design methods and strategies that can intervene in and direct the development of the landscape. Landscape architecture considers the landscape as a composition of natural, cultural, urban and architectonic elements in relation to ecological, social and economic parameters, and can be understood by means of morphological research.[1] According to this way of thinking, there is a relationship between content and form. Content is everything that comprises the landscape architectonic object – its material, topographic, technical, cultural and economic substance. Form involves the way in which the parts are assembled into a composition.[2]

This 'Delft approach' is characterized by theories, methods and techniques converging towards design research (analysis of existing designs or precedents) and research by design (formulation of new designs), and can be understood as a variable relationship between object and context.[3] In fact, the two methods cannot be seen apart from each other: design research is an indispensable step in research by design. From this point of view, we can consider this approach as a form of heuristics (way to find), a science that leads to new discoveries and inventions by taking a methodical approach.[4] The process of design research and research by design constitutes the following activities,[5] and is exemplified by graphic representations derived from research and design. The profile of landscape architecture at Delft is made up of three constituent domains, interrelating research and education:

- Architecture and Landscape continues to develop the theoretical and methodological bases by investigating contemporary landscape-based architecture, the use of new methods and techniques such as GIS and other advanced software, and the role of mapping/drawing in landscape architectonic research and design (5.1 and 5.2).

- Dutch Lowlands addresses the implicit architectural quality of man-made polder-scapes, the Dutch lowlands seen as a design laboratory to tackle worldwide questions of water management, and the Fine Dutch Tradition as a framework for landscape design that ingrates civil engineering, architecture and urban development (5.3 and 5.4).
- Urban Landscapes explores landscape as form and artefact of the urban realm, dealing with constructed open spaces within the city, landscape structure, underlying urban patterns, the landscape of urban hinterlands, and the interstitial spaces between cities; landscape is seen as that what lies underneath, the site or substratum, which is the point of departure for all design and planning (5.5 and 5.6).

Within these academic contexts, visual representations such as drawings, maps and virtual models are considered as a graphic form of research. Graphic knowledge offers landscape architects wide-ranging operative instruments for research and design. They function as devices for visual thinking and visual communication, and include analysis and presentation.[6] They are vehicles to communicate specific information for visual exploration and thinking on paper, and/or can express a vision. For us, visual representation is a fundamental tool in research and education, and serves as a generator for creativity in which different sorts of media can be employed, ranging from hand-drawing to geographic information systems.

Notes

1 Steenbergen, C.M. and Reh, W. *Architecture and Landscape: The Design Experiment of the Great European Gardens and Landscapes*, revised and expanded edn. Basel, Boston, Berlin: Birkhäuser, 2003.
2 Steenbergen, C.M., Meeks, S. and Nijhuis, S. *Composing Landscapes: Analysis, Typology and Experiments for Design*. Basel, Boston, Berlin: Birkhäuser, 2008.
3 De Jong, T. and Van der Voordt, D.J.M., eds. "Criteria for scientific study and design," in *Ways to Study and Research Urban, Architectural and Technical Design*. Delft: Delft University Press, 2002, pp. 19–30.
4 Steenbergen, C.M., Mihl, H. and Reh, W. "Introduction: design research, research by design," *Architectural Design and Composition*. Bussum, the Netherlands: Thoth Uitgeverij, 2002, pp. 12–25.
5 Steenbergen *et al.*, 2008, *op. cit.*
6 Nijhuis, S. "Landscape architecture: theory, methods and techniques." Delft University of Technology, 2010 (internal report).

Further reading

Bobbink, I. *Land InSight: A Landscape Architectonic Exploration of Locus*. Amsterdam: Sun Publishers, 2009.
Nijhuis, S. "Landscape architecture and GIS: geographic information science in landscape architectonic research and design." PhD thesis, Delft University of Technology, 2012.
Nijhuis, S., Van Lammeren, R. and Van der Hoeven, F. *Exploring the Visual Landscape. Advances in Landscape Physiognomic Research in the Netherlands*. Amsterdam: IOS Press, 2011.

Steenbergen, C.M. and Reh, W. *Urban Landscapes*. Basel, Boston, Berlin: Birkhäuser, 2011.

Steenbergen, C.M., Reh, W., Nijhuis, S. and Pouderoijen, M.T. *The Polder Atlas of the Netherlands. Pantheon of the Low Lands*. Bussum, the Netherlands: Thoth Uitgeverij, 2009.

Steenbergen, C.M., Van der Velde, R., Bobbink, I. and Nijhuis, S. *Research Programme, Urban Landscape Architecture 2006–2012*. Delft University of Technology, 2010.

de Wit, S. *Dutch Lowlands*. Amsterdam: Sun Publishers, 2009.

de Wit, S. and Aben, R. *The Enclosed Garden*. Rotterdam: 010 Publishers, 1999.

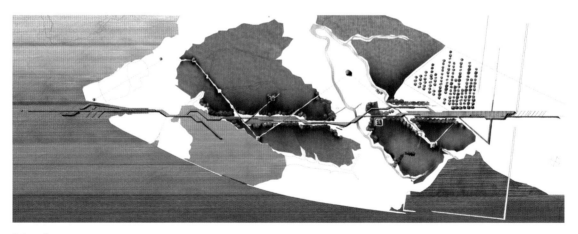

5.1 a–d
Design for a nature research centre and park in De Biesbosch, the Netherlands. (a–c) Section and plan, drawn by computer in two phases: first drawing map outline and elevation with a CAD program; second graphic processing with a vector and image-processing program. (d) Perspective, drawn digitally in two phases: first construction and rendering with a 3D modelling program; second graphic processing with an image-processing program. By Ioannis Tsoukalas, Mai Yoshitake and Robert Mayr.

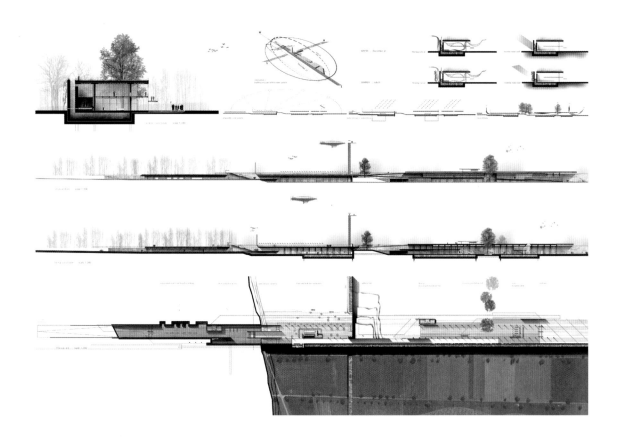

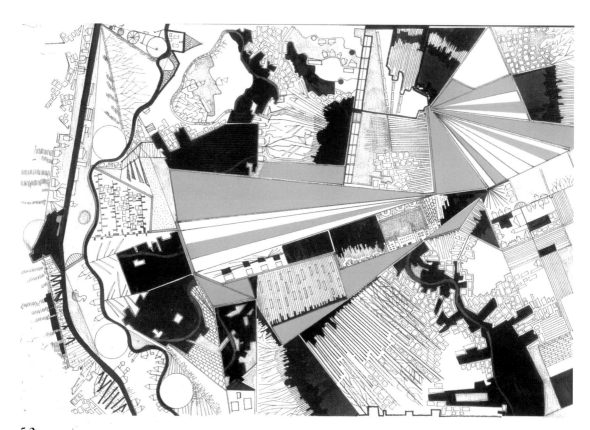

5.2
Revealing the hidden geometry of a landscape north of Utrecht (the Netherlands) by means of research by drawing.
Hand-drawn on tracing paper using drafting pens of different thickness. Green highlighting with coloured carton board.
By Lisa Troiano.

5.3 a–c

Multiple readings of a typical Dutch landscape by means of extraction and montage. Produced by hand, by cutting out and pasting fragments into parts of a scanned (hand-drawn) map and textures, which were modified by an image-processing program and printed on carton board. Red highlighting with coloured carton board. By Filippo Abrami.

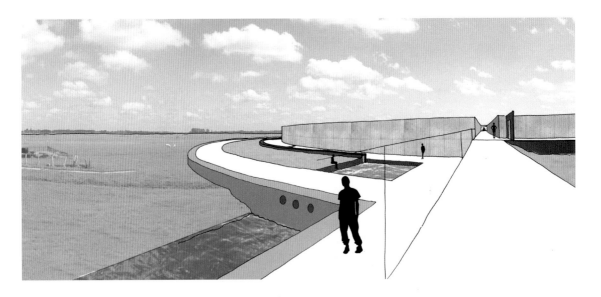

5.4 a–b
Design of a water-retention park in the polder landscape of Midden-Delfland, the Netherlands. Perspective drawn in two phases: first hand-drawn, based on computer-generated 3D model (a); second graphic processing with an image-processing program (b). By Marita Koch.

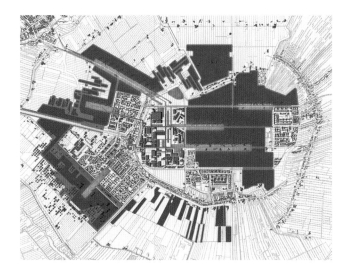

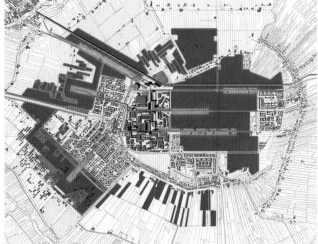

5.5 a–c
Design of a new
polder city in the
Ronde Venen,
the Netherlands.
Development of the
landscape in phases.
(a) Perspective drawn
by computer with a
CAD program, using
a digital topographic
map as background;
construction and
rendering of 3D
elements in CAD
program. (b) Plan
drawn by computer
with a CAD program
using a digital
topographic map
as background. (c)
Rendering with CAD
program. By Diego
Luna Quintanilla.

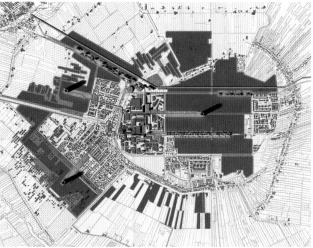

5.6 a–g
Design of a super
dike, where city
and landscape melt
together in the
polder Ronde Venen,
the Netherlands.
Perspective series
and development
drawing. Drawn by
computer in two
phases: first drawing
outline of map
and elevation with
a CAD program;
second graphic
processing with a
vector and image-
processing program.
By Minije Si.

6 Student Work View
Master planning

Kongjian Yu

Against a background of fast urbanization, China today is facing major challenges including wetland degradation, habitat destruction, loss of native biodiversity, flooding and drought, and a natural and cultural heritage and cultural landscape that is under pressure. Our team at the Graduate School of Landscape Architecture, Peking University has paid close attention to these problems and tried to find solutions.

Landscape design should be in harmony with nature and humans, with the knowledge of understanding all processes that affect the land. Based on this principle, a "negative planning approach"[1] is being developed against conventional urban planning schemes that ignore inherent land processes. The result is an ecological infrastructure based on a structural landscape network composed of essential landscape elements and both existing and potential spatial patterns that are of strategic significance in safeguarding critical natural, biological and cultural processes. These processes are critical in securing the integrity and identity of the natural and cultural landscapes, and in securing natural capital that supports sustainable ecosystem services.[2,3]

Design and planning should not be artificial and arbitrary. We emphasize that environmental, social and other considerations should be integrated into the design process. A methodological framework for design, created by Carl Steinitz (Harvard University, Department of Landscape Architecture, Graduate School of Design), is utilized to guide our design and planning. Steinitz emphasizes that we must be able to work at several scales of resolution in space and classification. Large-scale projects should focus on more scientific problems, and new technologies (such as GIS) will be used in design to analyze and resolve large, complex problems.

One important function of GIS is to manage spatial data. As all data are located in coordinate space, we can integrate different scales and different formats into a platform. Then we can use processes and tools offered by the platform for data analysis. Data preparation may include digitizing paper maps; in the Grand Canal project, students digitized ancient maps and tried adjusting them using modern surveying and mapping information. Such work may be arduous and sometimes boring, but it can help students to understand the principles of GIS.

Innovative methods are also used for evaluating various kinds of landscape processes: hydrology, biology, culture and recreation. For instance, we may use a flooding model to identify an area of flooding and evaluate a region's hydrological processes. We also use historical land-use data to evaluate how a region's visual quality has changed. In a more complex case, we may integrate data sources, processing them into one model using ArcGIS ModelBuilder, a useful tool that enables parameter values to be changed and the results visualized immediately. To give just one example, for a project identifying a giant panda dispersal corridor network, this tool is used to build a complicated model to evaluate the panda's habitat suitability.

GIS tools that simulate dynamic processes can also be used for impact evaluations when we change the landscape. These can be useful for comparing alternatives and obtaining immediate feedback on interactions when we make designs. As planning and design become more and more complicated, we should make our planning results more intelligible. We encourage students to utilize SketchUp, Google Earth and ArcScene to create 3D model visualizations. Planning results with 3D models can represent planning impacts intuitively, so they are easily understood by the public and decision-makers. These results help them participate in the planning and design process, and can have a real impact on decisions made.

Notes

1   Kongjian Yu, Li Dihua, Han Xili and Liu Hailong. "On the 'negative planning'". *City Planning Review*, 9, 2005, pp. 64–69.
2   Kongjian Yu, Li Dihua, Liu Hailong and Han Xili. "The growth pattern of Taizhou city based on ecological infrastructure: the negative approach to physical urban pattern." *City Planning Review*, 9, 2005, pp. 76–80.
3   Kongjian Yu, Li Dihua and Chao Luomeng. "Ten landscape strategies to build urban ecological infrastructure." *Planners*, 6, 2001, pp. 9–13.

What is the future of Beijing?

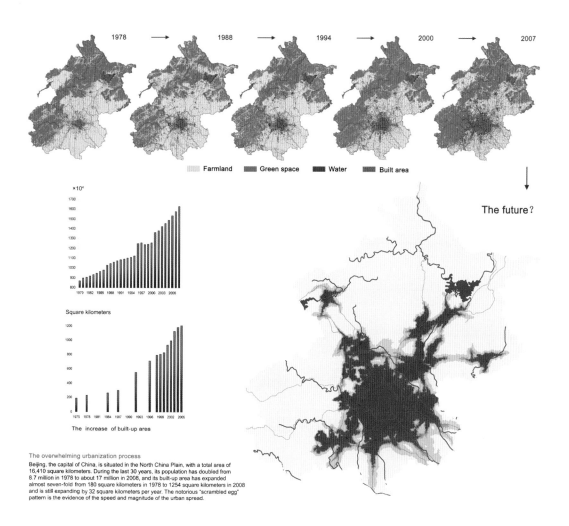

6.1

Beijing ecology security pattern strategy. Mapping the overwhelming urbanization process in Beijing, China. Regional mapping and diagramming images. During the past thirty years, the population of Beijing has doubled from 8.7 million in 1978 to about 17 million in 2008, and its built-up area has expanded almost seven times from 180 km² in 1978 to 1254 km² in 2008, and is still expanding by 32 km² per year. Created using AutoCAD, Illustrator and Photoshop. By Wang Sisi, Li Chunbo and Sun Qi.

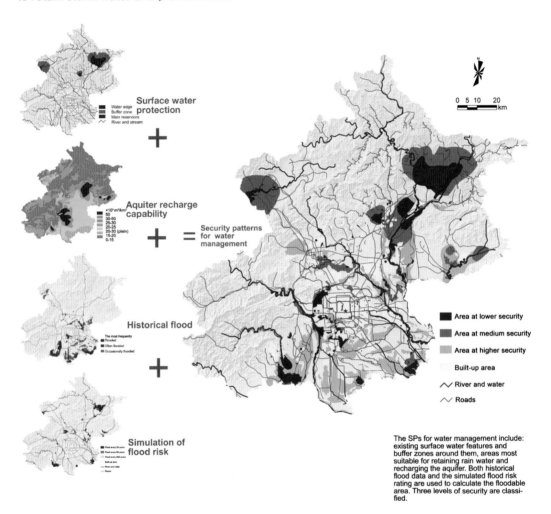

Security patterns for water management to retain storm water and prevent flood

Surface water protection
- Water edge
- Buffer zone
- Main reservoirs
- River and stream

+

Aquifer recharge capability
×10⁴ m³/km²
- 50
- 30-50
- 25-30
- 20-25
- 20-30 (plain)
- 15-20
- 0-15

+ =

Security patterns for water management

+

Historical flood
The most frequently
- Flooded
- Often flooded
- Occasionally flooded

+

Simulation of flood risk
- Flood every 20 years
- Flood every 50 years
- Flood every 200 years
- Built-up area
- River and water
- Roads

- Area at lower security
- Area at medium security
- Area at higher security
- Built-up area
- River and water
- Roads

The SPs for water management include: existing surface water features and buffer zones around them, areas most suitable for retaining rain water and recharging the aquifer. Both historical flood data and the simulated flood risk rating are used to calculate the floodable area. Three levels of security are classified.

0 5 10 20 km

6.2

Mapping security patterns for water management to retain storm water and prevent flooding. Both historical flood data and the simulated flood risk rating were used to calculate the floodable area providing habitat for specific bird species during the spring, summer and fall seasons. Created using AutoCAD, Illustrator and Photoshop. By Wang Sisi, Li Chunbo and Sun Qi.

Regional ecological infrastructure

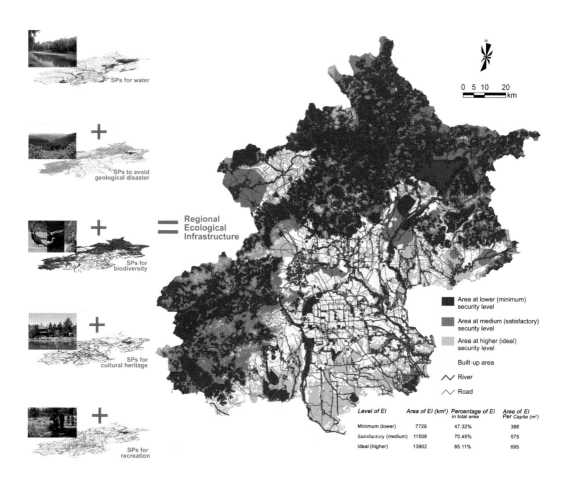

SPs for water

SPs to avoid geological disaster

Regional Ecological Infrastructure

SPs for biodiversity

SPs for cultural heritage

SPs for recreation

Area at lower (minimum) security level

Area at medium (satisfactory) security level

Area at higher (ideal) security level

Built-up area

River

Road

Level of EI	Area of EI (km²)	Percentage of EI in total area	Area of EI Per Capita (m²)
Minimum (lower)	7729	47.32%	386
Satisfactory (medium)	11508	70.45%	575
Ideal (higher)	13902	85.11%	695

6.3
Regional ecological infrastructure. Using an overlaying technique to integrate the security patterns for individual processes, alternatives for regional ecological infrastructure were developed at various quality levels: high, medium and low. These were used as a structural framework to guide and frame urban growth. Created using AutoCAD, Illustrator and Photoshop. By Wang Sisi, Li Chunbo and Sun Qi.

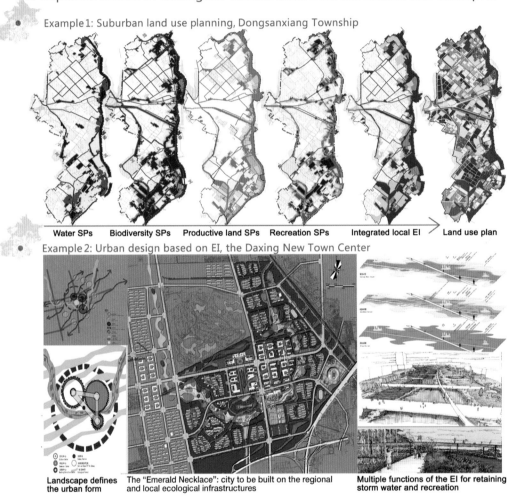

The implementation of ecological infrastructure across scales: two examples

Example 1: Suburban land use planning, Dongsanxiang Township

Water SPs   Biodiversity SPs   Productive land SPs   Recreation SPs   Integrated local EI   Land use plan

Example 2: Urban design based on EI, the Daxing New Town Center

Landscape defines   The "Emerald Necklace": city to be built on the regional   Multiple functions of the EI for retaining
the urban form   and local ecological infrastructures   storm water and recreation

6.4

Implementation of ecological infrastructure across scales. Various diagrams and maps to show ecological and infrastructural land use. The important urban design strategy is to build the city based on the regional and local ecological infrastructures. Created using AutoCAD, Illustrator and Photoshop. By Wang Sisi, Li Chunbo and Sun Qi.

THE COMPOSITION OF THE GRAND CANAL CULTURAL LANDSCAPE

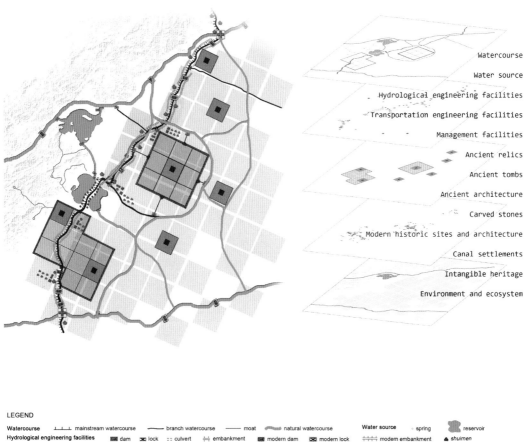

Watercourse

Water source

Hydrological engineering facilities

Transportation engineering facilities

Management facilities

Ancient relics

Ancient tombs

Ancient architecture

Carved stones

Modern historic sites and architecture

Canal settlements

Intangible heritage

Environment and ecosystem

LEGEND

Watercourse	⊥⊥⊥ mainstream watercourse	⎯ branch watercourse ⎯⎯ moat 〰 natural watercourse	Water source · spring 🏯 reservoir
Hydrological engineering facilities	🔲 dam ⊠ lock ∷ culvert 🔱 embankment 🔲 modern dam ⊠ modern lock ┼┼┼┼ modern embankment ⛵ shuimen		
Transportation engineering facilities	🏠 dock 🏠 modern dock •• qiandao ✚ yunkou ✚ modern yunkou		
Management facilities	⌓⌓ wall ⛵ warehouse ▬ ancient goverment ♦ qian ☺chaoguan 🔲 post house 🔲 modern historic sites and architecture		
🔲 ancient architecture ● ancient relics 🔲 carved stones ⬛ ancient tombs	🔲 canal settlement ▬ historical block	∘ other related ancient architecture/caves/tombs/relics	

6.5

Composition of the Grand Canal – a linear cultural landscape, the result of lengthy evolution driven by both human and natural processes. Watercourses, water sources, hydrological engineering facilities, transportation facilities and management facilities all affected the proper functioning of the Grand Canal. Created using AutoCAD, Illustrator and Photoshop. By Xi Xuesong, Chen Lin and Xu Liyan (this project won an American Society of Landscape Architects Student Award).

REGISTRATION OF THE GRAND CANAL HERITAGE IN JINING SECTION

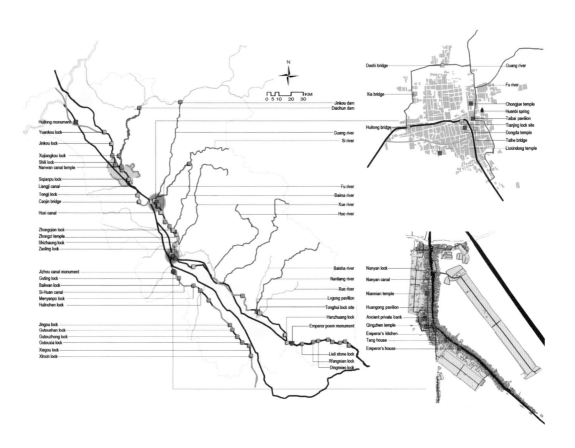

6.6

Registration of the Grand Canal heritage in Jining section. Nodal mapping and diagrams using AutoCAD, Illustrator and Photoshop. After verification of the previous step, predetermined heritage sites that meet the "three coincidence principle" were eventually identified and registered as the Grand Canal heritage site. By Xi Xuesong, Chen Lin and Xu Liyan (this project won an American Society of Landscape Architects Student Award).

7 Landscape Graphics

Neil Challenger and Jacqueline Bowring

As part of the teaching philosophy of the School of Landscape Architecture (SoLA) at Lincoln University, New Zealand, we cover a wide range of graphic media, from digital approaches to hybrid techniques using both digital and hand-drawn graphics, through to highly expressive drawing and painting. Our setting in Aotearoa (New Zealand) inspires us to develop graphic approaches that respond to the uniqueness of the cultural and natural landscapes. Although over eighty-five per cent of New Zealanders live in "urban" areas, it is often within non-urban areas where landscape architects are most involved – the landscapes of tourism, agriculture, infrastructure and communities.

Our key emphasis is on the space between computer-generated imagery and hand-drawn graphics, and we think of this as a new and potent zone. Echoing landscape architecture's foundational fusion of science and art, this "space between" acknowledges the role of the technological alongside that of the expressive in working with the landscape. Technology offers the potential to convey complexity, in terms of both spatial and temporal dimensions, while the expressive capacity of hand-drawn elements infuses graphics with a human quality. Alongside this, graphics are not simply for communication, but are also part of the design process itself – and for this reason the combination of media allows for a richer engagement with the site and the design development. Therefore the physical infrastructure of our teaching studios and our teaching philosophy is geared towards this space between the purely digital or the purely hand-drawn.

As a means of fostering drawing as an integral part of design, SoLA has reasserted the role of the sketchbook. Throughout the studio programme students are required to keep a sketchbook, and by making this mandatory we seek to establish the discipline of exploratory drawing as part of designing. Sketchbooks are used on field tours to record sites visually and to naturalize the act of drawing as a tool for understanding. In such settings, drawing becomes analytical as much as simply surveying the scene, and through the prolonged engagement that drawing demands, the mind penetrates the site more deeply than with the momentary act of photography. In the studio, the sketchbook becomes a tool for communication with tutors, where students can trace the evolution of their ideas rather than resorting to verbal descriptions that lose a grounding in place.

Drawing in a sketchbook also expands students' repertoire of media, providing a cheap and portable alternative to the digital tools that dominate today's world. The sketchbook is a place in which messiness, scribbles, doodles and trains of thought can unfold easily. While digital media can often be deceptive in terms of the apparent level of design development – with graphic sophistication sometimes a substitute for design resolution – the sketchbook is clearly about work in progress; it emphasises that design is about process, not just product.

Having a sketchbook is also a very useful starting point for students in responding to an increasing requirement for a greater analytical base to their designs. This requires them to express and develop their design and site planning decisions using analytical diagrams that explain the site and the rationales for its design, both using the process tool of the sketchbook and in developed design arguments of the finished drawing. This is not a rejection of "creativity", but rather an assertion of the cyclical and reflexive nature of design practice and an attempt to revalidate this using analytical and programmatic rigour. The result is to bring to light the programmatic and design drivers that are frequently lost from view below the drawing's surface, the invisibility of which has given the design work carried out by many students a slippery ephemerality as their designs were changed without meaningful regard for the rationales that should have been their foundation. This slipperiness is, of course, exciting and can be rewarding, but often it is frustrating and time-consuming, and the use of diagramming is intended to mediate a route between the perceived freedom of unconstrained design and the potential rigidity of analysis.

The examples illustrated here cover the continuum from wholly digital, as in Jonathan Turner's montage, to Lisa Fleming's hand-drawn graphics. Across the spectrum, these examples successfully address landscape architecture's representational challenges, from the "reading" and communication of place, constructing the argument, through to the fine detail of the site itself. The final, capstone studio, from which most of these examples are drawn, covers the classical landscape architectural approach, first engaging with the wider landscape context, moving down to the scale of the site in its setting, and then into 1:100 to explore the design up close. Matt Durning's broad-scale illustrations demonstrate how a richly layered graphic approach can convey a range of complex information relating to a site. Using a combination of plans, bird's-eye views, diagrams, colour charts and iconic imagery, Matt synthesises biophysical, cultural and experiential information to provide a comprehensive and compelling overview of Tekapo.

Matthew Tidball's graphics are also an evocation of place, and simultaneously express inspiration and design response. Using a combination of hand graphics, archaeological survey drawings and photographs, Matthew traces the evolution of his design from the almost invisible traces of prior presences on this site. The mixed media are combined in a way that is suggestive of the emotional and phenomenological aspects of the landscape, recognizing Maoris' centuries-old engagement with the landscape that extends into spiritual, mythological and metaphysical dimensions. This is also achieved very effectively in Lisa Fleming's work, which develops a proposal for a Maori stargazing project, something that requires the graphics to embody the sublime and intangible dimensions of the world of astronomy and myth. Lisa's sensitive yet strong black-and-white drawings are well tuned to the nocturnal world of stargazing, and demonstrate how layers of meaning and mythology could be incorporated into the site.

The hybridizing of digital and hand-drawn media is also used effectively by James McLean in his overlaying of the vision for the site onto the existing situation. Reminiscent of Gordon Cullen's townscape sequencing,[1] James journeys around Matakohe, indicating the various subtle interventions that would amplify the experience of the place. Using graphics in this way reminds us that, however familiar we might be with reading plans, our experience of the landscape is inevitably vertical, moving through the landscape gathering impressions and sensations. Matt Durning's detailed design drawings also illustrate the combination of plan and perspective, and expand into the temporal dimension of a night experience. Tekapo is famous for its observatories and is currently advocating for the creation of a World Night Sky Reserve to protect celestial darkness, and Matt's nocturnal drawings reflect this.

Note

1   Cullen, G. *The Concise Townscape.* Oxford: Architectural Press, 1961.

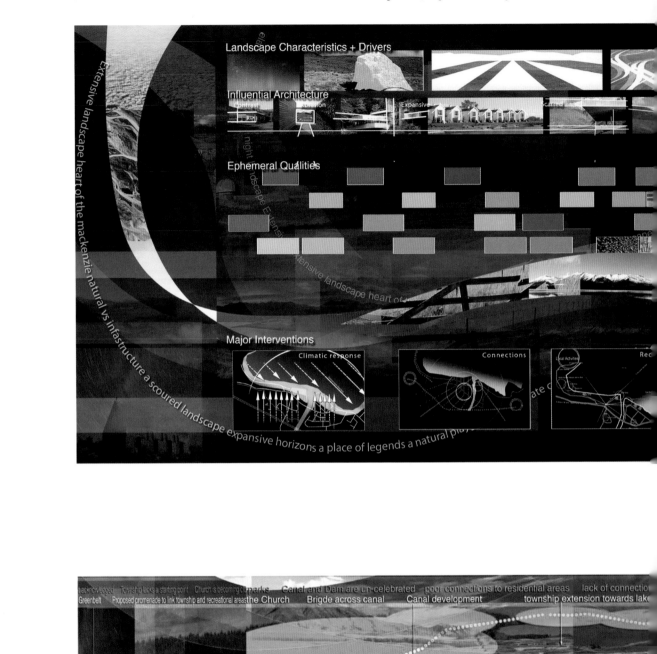

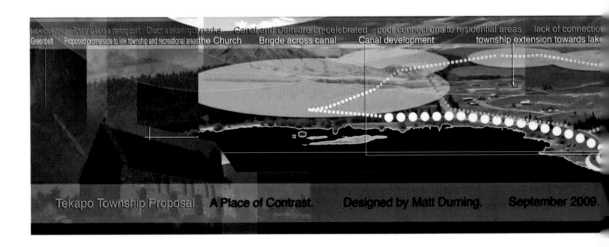

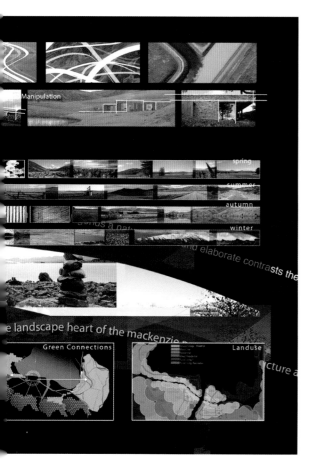

7.1

Broad-scale argument – site character, analysis and inspiration for the redevelopment of Tekapo, an existing tourist village in New Zealand's Southern Alps. Part of plan 1 (of 6), original approximately 8 × 17"; Adobe Photoshop. The plan distils the site's key characteristics, such as colour, seasonality, landscape structure and drivers, into an evocative, accessible and inspirational graphic statement that is a clear, informative and very usable evocation of the site. By Matt Durning.

7.2

Broad-scale structure – site structure and connection to surrounding landscape for the redevelopment of Tekapo, an existing tourist village in New Zealand's Southern Alps. Part of plan 1 (of 6), original approximately 5 × 25"; Adobe Photoshop. Using oblique aerial and diagramming graphics, the image captures the scale and openness of the site in a way that is informative as to its structure, form and three-dimensional character. By Matt Durning.

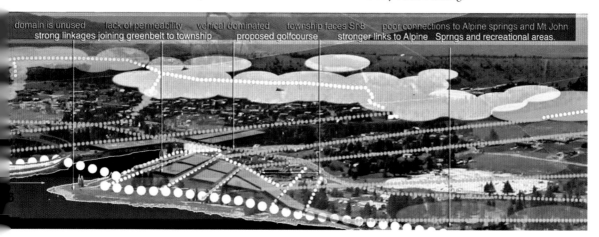

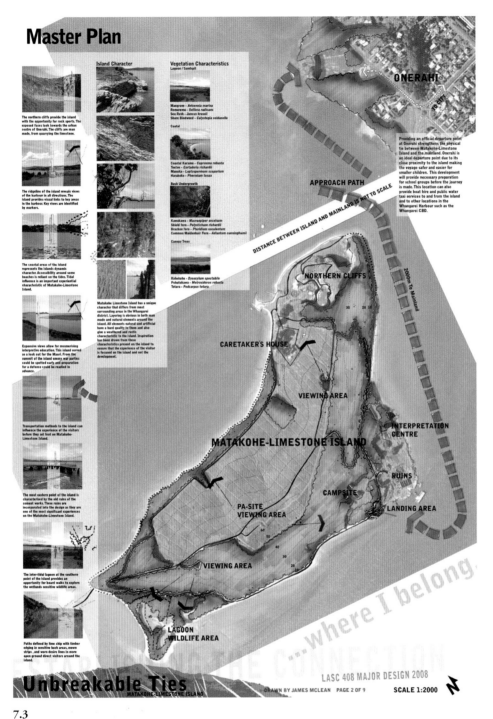

Master plan and serial vision for an outdoor pursuit centre on Matakohe Island, far north New Zealand. Plan 2 of 9, original 34 × 24"; plan and sketches hand-drawn and rendered, recombined as photomontage/plan in Adobe Photoshop. The plan view shows "where" things happen; "what" happens is shown using overlain photos that both describe the island's character and provide a detailed serial vision of the proposed development. By James McLean.

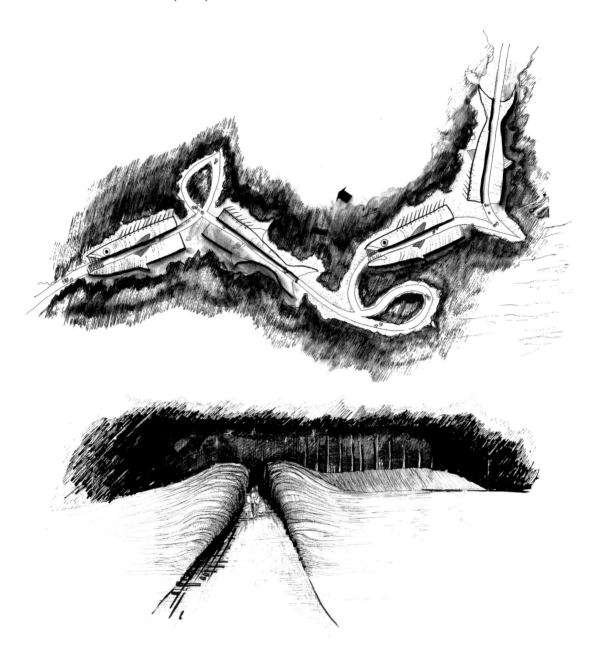

7.4
Detailed design (1:100), plan and sketch for a Maori stargazing project at Mangamaunu in New Zealand's South Island.
Part of plan 5 (of 5), original approximately 18 × 10''; pen and ink. Careful applications of black-and-white graphics
reflect the site's nocturnal use, which, with the rich narrative of the plan and the visceral sketch, creates a nuanced and
layered graphic richly expressive of its first-nation client. By Lisa Fleming.

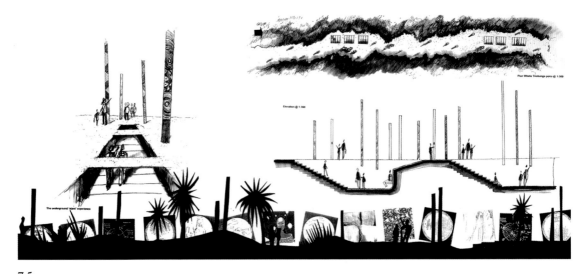

7.5
Detailed design (1:100), plan, sketch, section and boarder graphic for a Maori stargazing venture at Mangamaunu in New Zealand's South Island. Part of plan 5 (of 5), original approximately 24 × 15''; pen-and-ink drawings, cut paper and photocopier reprographics. The layered images, surprisingly rich in detail, strongly express the cultural character and experiential quality of the proposal in a way that resonates with site and client. By Lisa Fleming.

7.6
Site illustration/perspective for a proposed brownfield town development in Petone in New Zealand's North Island. Part of plan 5 (of 6), original approximately 12 × 20''; Adobe Photoshop collage and mashup. The illustration eclectically pulls together images, materials, buildings and people to describe crisply and accessibly the proposal's riverside experience. The image's vibrant colours, layering and quirkiness combine to give the drawing a playful sense. By Jonathan Turner.

8 Drawing the Landscape

Richard Weller

The past twenty years has seen the emergence of digital technologies as the predominant medium of representation used today. Schools and practices everywhere have had to negotiate the millennial transition from graphite to silicon. Whole schools have had to decide on their representational emphasis, and re-tool. A whole generation of 'pencil-pushers' can barely talk to their students about the technology that lies behind their graphics. In dark corners, students effectively teach themselves the latest tricks. Students need to get in control of these machines, whereas at the moment the machine still has the upper hand. Like Formula 1 vehicles, computers can do what we could never do with our bodies, but when one misjudges a line, the consequences can be spectacularly dire. Students need to learn to sketch and think with computers, instead of mind-numbingly rendering another meaningless bombastic vista to nothing in particular. Similarly, the new wave of diagramming and mapping, while sometimes drawing out genuinely new information about the way the world works, is often aesthetic exotica suspended in its own cybernetic ether.

We can, I think, look forward to computer programs that really serve thought and art, and better approximate ecological and urban complexity. With generative programs, we are already seeing designs emerge from animations of certain types of processes, but I have not included these as they are not yet, strictly speaking, within students' range. What I have tried to do with this selection of work from the University of Western Australia is map out this period of transition from graphite to silicon and, through a range of media, highlight some representational issues of both a practical and perhaps philosophical nature.

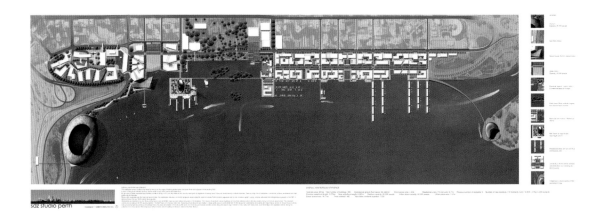

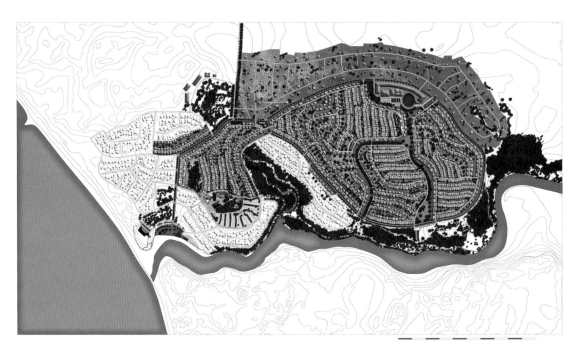

8.1 and 8.2

These two plans, one of an urban waterfront development and the other of a suburban masterplan, strike a fine balance between the real and the hyper-real. Both subtly mix swatches of material and colour from real aerial photographs with colour and materials from the computer. The drawings both differentiate clearly between the proposed and the existing, and show with great accuracy the massing of built form and distribution of open spaces. In professional work, suburban and urban design projects require accurate representation to be believable, but as a consequence projects can appear mechanistic, which alienates both the client and the public. These drawings are believable and, through colour and attention to detail, they are also a marketable and visually attractive drawings. By Esti Nagy (8.1) and Julia Robinson (8.2).

8.3

This image of an urban design concept for Dubai does well to avoid the excessive detail of hyper-reality and retain a sketch-like quality. As opposed to naturalism, all the materials and objects are overtly fake (virtual). However, to avoid a completely flat, robotic image, the surfaces are rendered in a way that mottles the colour and texture so as to enliven the image. The use of colour is restrained and highlights the features of the concept. Instead of labouring to produce an ersatz reality, this image retains the freshness of an idea – a proposition not a resolution. This technique of sketching with a computer is also fast and therefore affordable. By Julian Bolleter.

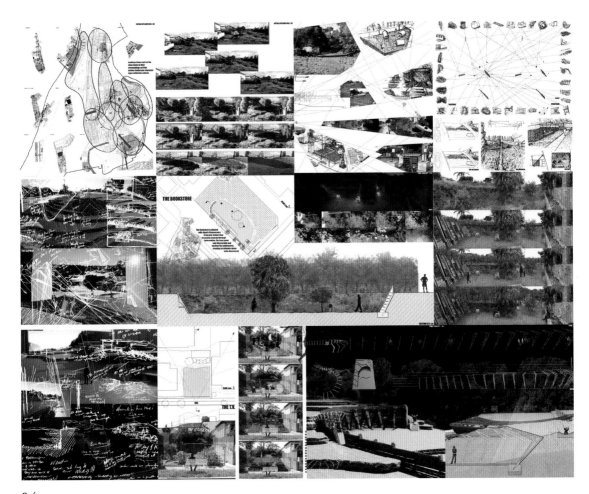

8.4

This is part of a creative process that begins with infinite possibility and ends with only one "scheme"; the most important drawings (scribbles) are the earliest. To maximize the development of the early phase of the design process, one needs to engage the hand and the brain in a messy and volatile feedback loop. The more "stuff" that is produced in this early phase, the better. In this montage, the student brings together a range of media as he records the process of teasing out his design approach to vacant wastelands in suburbia. By Alex Fossilo.

8.5

The idea for this project in Queens Square in Brooklyn was that the surrounding city was a vortex and the public open space is the still point. Instead of contouring down into the earth, as one would expect of a real vortex, here the public space terraces upwards. Through opacity and releasing objects from fixity (one of whom is Dorothy from *The Wizard of Oz*), the whole image is choreographed to express the design's intended energy. By Tom Griffiths.

8.6

To record and test ideas quickly, composing a series of rudimentary perspectival sketches is a necessary skill. Often these are most effective as mere doodles, but hand-drawn presentation images can also be produced. In this case, the drawing is clearly more than a doodle: it is an example of a compelling presentation sketch and, while this sort of thing can be learned, some individuals are predisposed to it. This drawing uses all the tricks of the trade: warped perspective, a full range of line weights and textures, a full gradation of grey tones, and a balanced but asymmetrical composition. Most importantly, it leaves things out so the viewer's mind can complete the picture. By Julia Robinson.

8.7 a–c
In this panel of three images, Richard Weller and Mike Rowlands attempt to communicate the sublime. The panel was part of a competition for a memorial to the victims of the 2004 Boxing Day tsunami. The images have been meticulously constructed in Photoshop to show the effects of lights set on the ocean's surface. More than anything, in order to stand out from hundreds of entries in a competition, the images had to work powerfully on a visceral level. This poster wastes no space on doing anything but conveying the raw emotion of the proposal, and as such it was successful. By Richard Weller with Mike Rowlands.

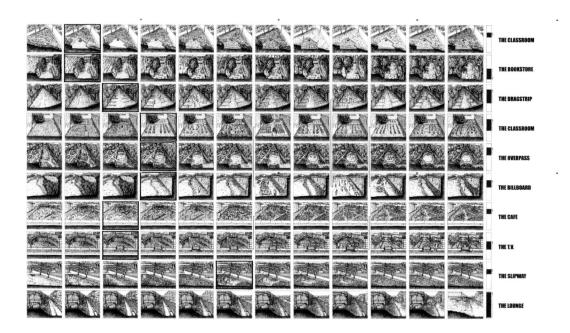

THE CLASSROOM
THE BOOKSTORE
THE DRAGSTRIP
THE CLASSROOM
THE OVERPASS
THE BILLBOARD
THE CAFE
THE T.V.
THE SLIPWAY
THE LOUNGE

8.8

We often hear that time is one of landscape architecture's most distinguishing qualities and yet, apart from the recent trend of producing long diagrammatic timelines to show the possible staging of a project and its increase in biota, there is still little representational attention to really engaging time in landscape imagery. This drawing introduces the problem of denoting time in landscape architecture. This sheet literally sketches out the possible lifelines of ten different, small, vacant sites in suburbia, sites where nothing much, apart from the flow of time, happens. The graphic technique is cinematic, that is, it is based on still frames spliced together. The changes from frame to frame are small and do not proffer some predetermined ideal direction. As a whole, the sheet itself becomes a quivering expression of moments. By Alex Fossilo.

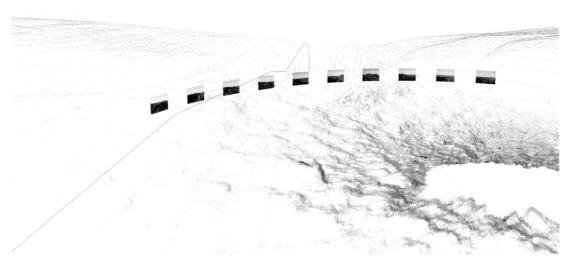

8.9
This drawing attempts to go beyond the conventional techniques of landscape representation (maps, contour plans and so on) to produce radically site-specific mappings as a basis for making its own site-specific architecture. The author uses sophisticated technologies currently employed by surveyors. The images contain maps and photos resulting from surveys of the site's vegetation using terrestrial laser scanning. Ten photos of the site are strategically incorporated into this CAD model of all the data from the scanning. By Ian Weir.

8.10
An exquisite hand-sketch study drawing of the subtle patterns and textures of the Australian bushland. Students are encouraged to learn the craft of drawing not as a form of nostalgia, but as a way of meditating on the world of light, a way of flattening the world, a way of dilating time and capturing space. By Bekk Crombie.

9 (In)Complete

Marc Miller and Jamie Vanucchi

It bears repeating that the process of creating a drawing or model is important for the individual to engage sites and to identify the associated "problematics", and then to invent specific solutions. The activities addressing these issues necessitate the generation of content, or recordings, documenting a process specific to the requirements of the problem and the interests of the designer(s). By default, it is the relationship of the recordings relative to the problematic, and the person who generated the recordings and the site, that creates opportunities for discovery and discourse. Those recordings seen as significant in the process may be described as artifacts, capable of describing particular parts of the process and creating significant relationships between other artifacts, revealing multivalent relationships and conditions. However, given the frequent default to procedural processes, including standardized methods of recording sites, the sole reliance on historic precedents or typologies, and the exclusive use of conventional drawing formats often has the effect of deterring critical thought and authentic problem-solving. Artifacts are subsequently structured in a manner akin to an operational manual, deterring revelatory moments in the process.

A more critical construction of recordings results in rhetorical structure, creating a framework or space in which the process and product can be altered to respond to the work. It is within this dynamic, reflexive and critical environment that multi-valent conditions are revealed within the project, and can be described as an operating environment versus an operational manual. When considered in this context, the entire body of work is activated and is more accurately described as a model, given that it is structured to address the process using the site as a testing ground. This also has the effect of transforming the artifact, bringing into question the intention of the project at a number of temporal scales and multi-site and project relationships. In short, the fabrication of two- and three-dimensional content may be used to reveal information unto itself and as part of a larger practice, capable of modification. The title "(In)Complete" refers to this necessity for the content to demonstrate an internal logic, and its capability of supporting larger relationships within the specific problematic and greater practice.

Here we consider this process as forms of models placing emphasis on the intention to create processes in which designers are able to identify methods of discovery and representation capable of being transported to other projects. We describe them as descriptive or performative, and capable of being expressed through representational drawings, digital visualizations and physical modeling. Most importantly, as operating environments, they are embedded in the processes, altering the nature of how the representational artifact is identified, and the content within the artifact.

The descriptive model is one that uses two- and three-dimensional media as a means to formulate an approach to a project. The process relies on manipulating conventional methods used to catalog sites, including orthographic projection, photography, and models to enable the designer to identify a problematic. Media produced as part of analysis become transformed through a process of iterative representation, ideally using the contrast method of recording (model to drawing). At all times, the designer is to be mindful of the natural processes they are representing, and subsequently transforming, throughout the process. In this manner, as the project becomes increasingly abstracted from the site, the processes of interest are revealed as a unique set of recordings that may be applied in the process of project development. The model is revealed in the manner in which existing processes are represented, transformed and applied as part of the project. Each recording relies on the next step to represent the process and project accurately, while also serving as a finished exploration of a unique part of the problematic.

The performative model takes a different approach to how ecological processes and relations are used in project development. In this instance, the interiority related to process favored in the descriptive model is suppressed through iterative mappings. Cross-scale systems mapping describes both the constructive/ordering and destructive/entropic processes shaping the site/system within a particular frame. The content within this analysis references geography only as a supporting characteristic, leveraging science-based applications of scale, including time to measure the site. The content produced as part of the modeling process is more accurately described as a set of visualizations, revealing conditions in the site that are not necessarily apparent. The model is constructed as these visualizations are layered, nested and extended, and becomes the framework that suggests both design intervention as a series of timed strategies, and methods and metrics to measure performance post-intervention(s). Interventions occur within the existing and projected timelines set by the pace of modeled processes. This enables the designer to project scenarios, but does not allow for certainty, so that the designer must embed some strategy for receiving and responding to system performance.

These images, by students in the Department of Landscape Architecture at Cornell University, represent analog and digital methods of representation from undergraduate studios generating descriptive or performative models. The representational artifacts that have been constructed create and support arguments that were intended to address specific questions generated from common problem sets, all of which serve as examples of (In)Complete representation.

9.1 a–d
Evolution park experience. Series representing varied park experience and program through time. Note that each perspective is keyed to a particular day and time so the student can plot conditions and develop the proposed program accordingly. By David Zielnicki.

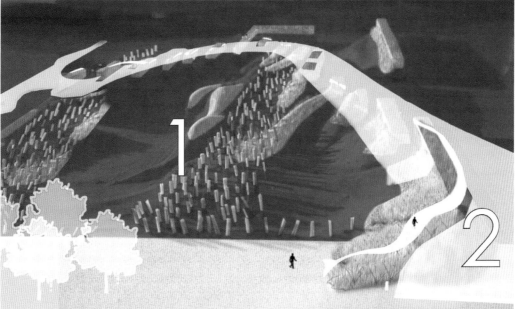

9.2 a–b
Shallow-water habitat study. Grappling with the four-dimensional character of these projects proves challenging for students. As the designs are always in a state of "becoming", choosing a time interval for representation is a significant step. Each process (e.g. deposition versus sea-level rise) has its own timeline and metric set, and the student must develop a proposal that accounts for the interaction of varying rates of change, via both human and non-human processes. By Maria Calderon.

9.3
Performance ground scenario development. This representation deals with the complexities of economic, social and environmental processes interacting over time. Design interventions consist of "plug-ins", or the punctuated influx of energy and resources at a particular site and time to redirect the existing web of processes toward increasingly positive impacts and outcomes. By Maria Hook and Aidan Chambliss.

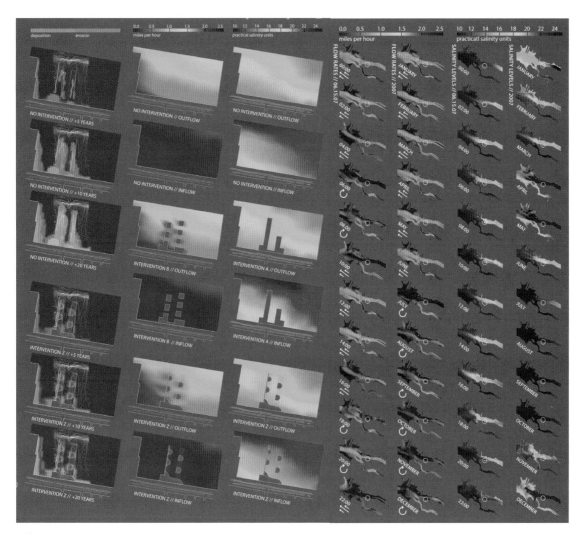

9.4

Colonization-site process. This exploratory series begins with a study of daily and annual changes in salinity and flow. Interestingly, after getting a handle on these processes, the student was unsure how to proceed. Under advisement, the student took an experimental approach by placing a form in the water, letting these processes interact with the form, and observing and recording the outcomes. By David Zielnicki.

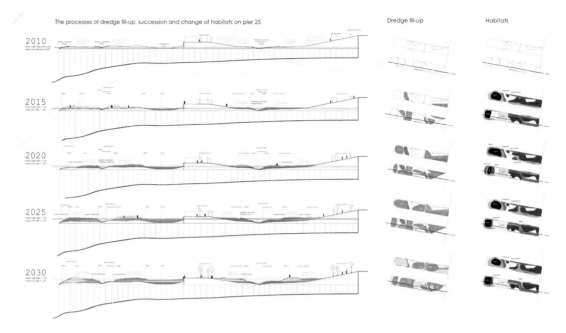

9.5 a–c

Succession, habitat and adaptive design scenario. This project begins with an exploration of the requirements of various human, fish and bird habitats (e.g. researcher/educator, killifish and swamp sparrow). Since the habitats on the piers are dependent on a relationship with water, the design is closely tied to tidal regime and sea-level rise, and uses dredge material from the Hudson River to generate a constantly changing and shifting environment. By Stina Hellqvist.

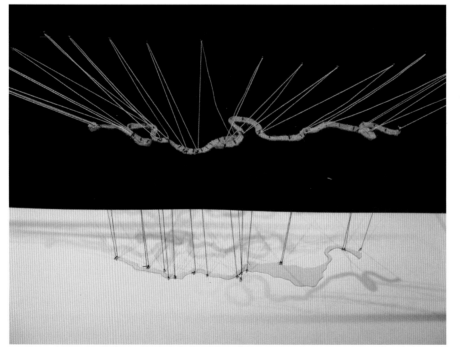

9.6

This model represents a transect taken around a water feature. The model illustrates change in elevation at a glance. Secondary information regarding how the landscape was broken up into separate spatial experiences is illustrated by the location of the armature supporting the wire. Time is marked on the rope, revealing the duration of the walk. By Anders Lindquist.

9.7 a–c
These excerpts from a drawing and model use a simple set of rules to create images illustrating surface conditions and
materiality. In the vector drawing, topographic conditions are imagined through slight changes in how materials are
represented through the use of patterns and layering. The drawings then serve as the basis for the model, which creates an
abstracted topographic surface. By Ulrike Simschitz.

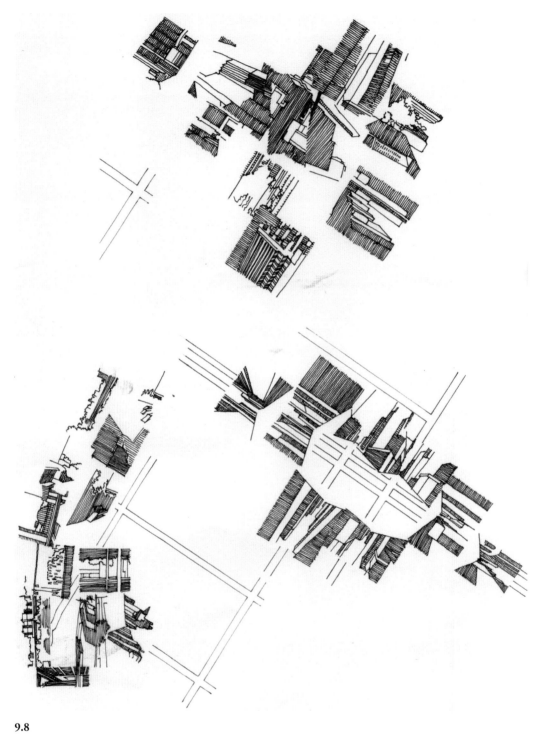

9.8
This drawing demonstrates the value of invention in drawing versus conventional drawing. The drawing narrates a walk taken in an urban environment using the street grid and scenographic patterning of buildings as an illustrative tool. By Aidan Chambliss.

10 Exactness and Abstraction in Landscape Architectural Reproduction

Roberto Rovira

Landscape architectural representation in the age of digital reproduction offers a powerful array of tools with which to model, reproduce and embellish in increasingly convincing ways. An emergence of sophisticated digital techniques has quickly found its way into design, and landscape architecture education and practice – although historically slower than other design disciplines to adapt to these tools – is poised to benefit from this exponentially increasing technological prowess. It is often more challenging to achieve realistic visual representation in landscape architecture than in other disciplines, such as architecture and interior design, where the depiction of space generally relies on the accurate representation of objects. Landscape offers other complexities, not least of which is the inherent dynamic of its elements and the very nature of ecology, which is fundamentally about understanding the set of ongoing relationships between organisms and their environment, and less about understanding discrete elements in isolation.

Because landscape architecture is almost invariably concerned with dynamic systems, connections and varying degrees of impermanence, one could argue that a digital segmentation and Cartesian simplification of its elements is counter to its very nature. Landscape is more about gradients and less about units. It is less about a calculus that divides geometries into infinitesimal parts, and more about the fluid and the indivisible. This distinction is most relevant when speaking about photorealistic visual communication, which attempts to render every last individual strand and reflection of light in pursuit of the ultimate simulacrum. It might eventually be possible, and sometimes desirable, to accomplish realistic exactitude in landscape representation, but the desire to replicate reality in landscape's visual communication often gets in the way of understanding, and ultimately communicating, its visceral and ineffable qualities. By embracing inexactness and even abstraction in visual rendering, landscape's inherent qualities and potential can be more fully explored and expressed without the usurping desire to treat every step of development as a final rendering.

When it comes to diagramming site analysis and inventory, however, current landscape education and practice has effectively appropriated sophisticated visual communication tools afforded by digital technology. Relieved of the need to analyze landscapes and ecologies with physical overlays and transparencies, digital tools facilitate prototyping and seriality of images that can quickly and effectively convey dynamic transformation, phasing and incrementation. Analytical comparisons and studies can be much more experimental in their approach, allowing the visualization of a multitude of options, which in themselves open the door to acute observations about a landscape that may have been harder to come by when constrained by physical drawing tools. McHarg would have reason to be happy and proud of his imprint and his legacy,[1] and might even be floored by the way landscape architects have sublimated analysis into the realm of art. Analysis diagrams, site plans and aerial photography are enhanced with telling illustrations and diagrams that convey important relationships, vectors, flows and corridors, for example. Context, siting, and the way in which a landscape fits into a larger system are effectively communicated diagrammatically, and in ways that depend less on realism and more on abstraction through overlays and drawings that are nevertheless quantitatively accurate. Analysis can be, and often is, beautiful with the aid of current digital tools.

Since the field of landscape architecture demands a process that is both sensory and analytical, its visual communication in the examples provided from Florida International University's Landscape Architecture Department aims to engage both realms. The concepts of time and transformation, which are essential to understanding landscapes and ecology, become particularly interesting subjects in a number of the compositions depicted. In all cases, emphasis is placed on saying the most with the least: text is kept to a minimum whenever possible; line weights and compositional strategies are stressed as they would be in a fine art drawing; students are challenged to reduce complex systems to their essential components in inventory and analysis diagrams. This economy of means is stressed as critical not only to convey essential information in typically complex sites, but also as a way to understand them better, given that it is only through an in-depth investigation of ideas that the more important attributes can be distilled into the fewest strokes.

Nonetheless, it is crucial to underscore that in all investigations pertaining to site in the examples presented, analog precedes digital. The final product may contain both; but the initial investigation is conducted as two- and three-dimensional exercises that emphasize materiality (stone, earth, vegetation, wood, etc.), and visual representation of the digital kind takes a back seat so that the primacy of material and the analog process is understood first-hand. In the examples dealing with the post-industrial landscapes of a limestone quarry in South Florida, for example, the qualities of a section of stone are studied in non-digital ways: its ability to filter and retain water is tested by filtering blue dye through its cross-section (10.3); its porosity and make-up is investigated by crushing and reassembling it (10.7); its propensity to break in un/predictable ways is explored (10.4). The objective of this approach is to impart a visceral sense to site and project, and to inform the final character and quality of visual representation.

Several examples of information design in landscape architecture are also included from a course whose aim was to synthesize digital drawing methods and once again attempt to convey clarity despite complexity, as seen in the drawing of the tree evolutions. The form and role of visual representation in landscape architecture is explored in these examples at a multiplicity of scales and via a multiplicity of means. The ability to draw vector line work with digital precision over expansive areas is especially valuable when it is essential to distill knowledge from information with accuracy. The sensory translation of site, material and space, via non-digital, inexact and imprecise means, however, proves equally critical in the examples provided. They demonstrate how digital and non-digital means of visual representation, investigation, design and communication are necessarily interdependent in expressing landscape architecture's often elusive, complex and ineffable qualities.

Note

1   McHarg, I. *Design with Nature*. New York: Doubleday/Natural History Press, 1971.

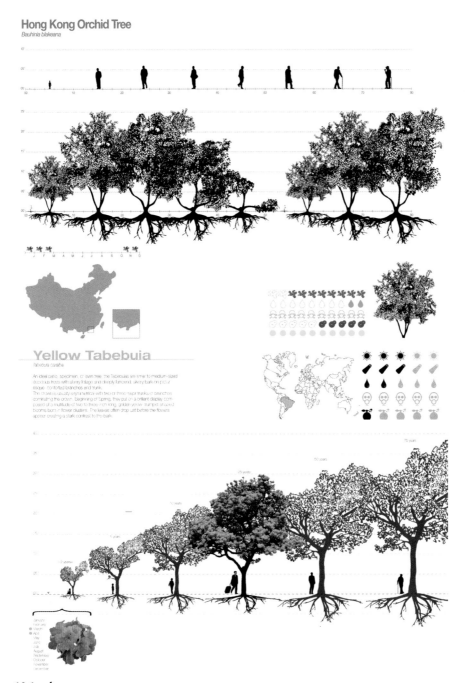

10.1 a–b

Tree evolution graphic: (a) black-and-white, collage profiles; (b) black-and-white with tree element in color, collage profiles. Students developed a graphic that represented the evolution of a tropical or subtropical tree over seventy-five years and referenced it against a human being in the same timeframe. The work communicates the species' particular attributes graphically, ranging from sun and salt tolerance to drainage requirements, seasonal attributes, toxicity and fragrance, among other qualities. By Joanna Ibarra (a) and Kevin Banogon (b).

Ephemeral Boundaries

10.2

Ephemeral boundaries, panel for Center for Land Use Interpretation. Includes a regional map, site analysis, diagrams, master plan, sections, overview aerial perspective and key captivating collage perspectives with descriptive text. Analog models depict the gradual migration of water over the landscape using wood, ink and wax models that progressively transform across their surfaces. Sections and perspectives are indicated on key plans (small size located below each drawing for reference). As a process to understand phenomenological space, the project proposes bringing back a natural system to educate the public about this unique area of South Florida, where urban sprawl meets the Everglades. The strategy of implementing boundaries as ephemeral and fluctuating was utilized throughout. The proposal solicited the creation of a Center for Land Use Interpretation – South Florida to provide better comprehension of Florida's natural environment, modeled after an institute by the same name in Culver City, California. Diagrams, key sections and marketable perspectives help communicate the feel and understanding of the site. By Brennan Baxley.

10.3

Post-industrial landscape for porous boundaries project. Beautifully crafted panel with well-laid-out collections of master plan, key plans, eye-catching collage perspectives, photos and sections to capture the essence of the post-industrial site. The natural grain of the Everglades has been shaped by thousands of years of hydro/geomorphology that has resulted in tree islands that are unique in their inverted teardrop form. These prominent landscape forms create habitats for flora and fauna that is unique to the South Florida region. The same watershed network that has shaped the land above-ground has also carved into the limestone bedrock, giving it a diagonal grain as it erodes and percolates through the porous slab into the aquifer. The referenced photos help depict these site qualities. By Sefora Chavarria.

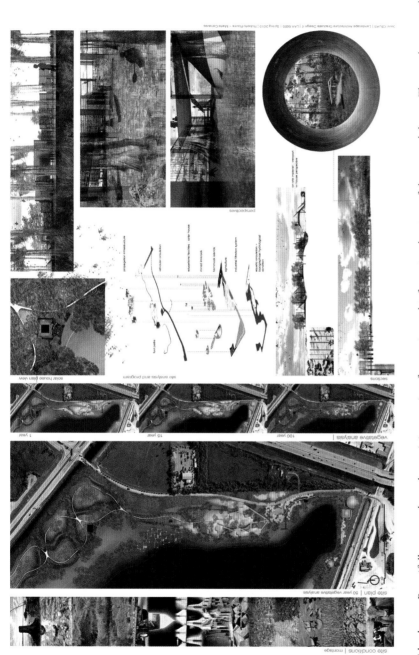

10.4

Post-industrial landscape. Beautifully arranged panel containing a series of expressive and informative drawings of the site and design. The area known as the "Lake Belt Region" in South Florida appears as a series of immense pools that are clearly identifiable from vehicular roadways such as Florida's Turnpike, as well as through satellite imagery. These large water bodies, notable for their bright blue-green color and orthogonal geometry, are the by-product of limestone mining operations in South Florida that date back to the turn of the twentieth century. This region currently serves as a barrier between one of our world's most diverse ecosystems, the Everglades, and the encroaching urban development of Miami, Florida. The scars left by the demands of urban development are revealed in these water-filled pits, which range in depth from 60 to 100 feet. The inherent qualities of a scar and the subsequent process of healing and mitigation are explored through the landscape in this project. Considering the magnitude of the site's existing quarries, further excavation might seem counterintuitive. These ideas are captured in the panel through small vignettes, large master plan (composed black-and-white aerial with proposed colored plan depicting intervention), and seductive perspective (using a play of opacity effects to capture transitional space and quality of forest and site). An exploded axo-plan, carefully placed in the center of the panel, depicts the systems and anatomy of the designed site. By Devin Cejas.

10.5

Post-industrial landscape. Beautifully arranged panel containing a series of expressive and informative drawings of the site and design. Clever balance between black-and-white with subtle color interventions. A large master plan in the center of the panel is the main focal point. Eye-catching perspectives capture the feel and character of the space, along with beautifully rendered section elevations. The drawings communicate the transformative effects that are triggered by human actions such as limestone quarrying and/or natural processes in the Lake Belt mining region in South Florida. The drawings also represent an alternative for the reclamation of a residual urban/industrial void based on the study of the concepts of disturbance/resistance and a thorough understanding of the geology and hydrology of the Everglades areas bordering the western edge of Miami. By Carolina Jaimes.

10.6

Post-industrial landscape. Well-composed, informative and visually appealing panel, containing a large master plan with supportive key drawings, including a series of striking digitally composed perspectives, well balanced with a series of sections. A small catalog of materials and textures, scanned and placed at the bottom left of the panel, helps describe the tactile qualities of the place. By Andres Pineda.

10.7

Post-industrial landscape for urban defragmentation project. Well-composed panel with a sequence of drawings including site analysis and diagrams, large master plan, and a series of key sections placed in the center of the panel to capture strategic elevational changes in the design and site. Diagrams created in Illustrator, arranged in grid layout, depict the systems and components of the plan (form and space development, circulation, tree canopy, urban farming and community gardens, water-edge conditions, cypress swamp, industrial park and faunas, pineland and collection). The pineland, community gardens, collections, urban farming, cypress swamp and industrial park are also handsomely rendered through collage perspective (in Photoshop). A catalog of plant materials is tiled and arranged on the panel for further communicative purposes. Detailed plan and sections also are part of the panel. By Luis Jiménez.

10.8

Qualitative measures crossing mimicry for urban ecology. Miami's Urban Development Boundary (a line established in the 1970s to limit westward sprawl): produced by digitally layering hand drawings of the curvilinear forms that characterize water flows in the Everglades using mud, over the development patterns evident in aerial photographs and plans. The drawing combines digital and non-digital techniques by superimposing the development patterns evident in aerial photographs and plans – the Cartesian subdivision of land – with the curvilinear forms that characterize water flows in the Everglades region. These two geometries are traced and subsequently juxtaposed over the land uses from which they are derived. Through this simple act of bringing these different ways of viewing and shaping the environment into the context of the aerial photograph, another example of the ongoing dialectic of city and nature is exposed. By Cecilia Hernandez.

11 Dioramic Modes
The critical potential of the diorama in the landscape architecture design process

Holly A. Getch Clarke with Max Hooper Schneider

The current research undertaken by myself and my students at Harvard Graduate School of Design focuses on the critical reclamation of repressed modes of imaging[1] promised by the diorama. Conventional design practices dismiss the diorama out of hand because of its prosaic, didactic and non-quantifiable origins, while paradoxically producing dioramic worlds through 3D digital modeling programs. Moreover, the diorama derives historically from cultural practices related to the fascination with landscape depiction in various forms.[2] "Dioramic modes" generate critical operations that expand beyond the view-oriented practices[3] of traditional diorama representation to introduce an impermanent, analog, three-dimensional construction and tactile manipulation of materials into spatial and environmental extent. The typical diorama operates through perspectival illusionism/realism, singularity, fixed time and material stasis. Instead, dioramic modes both challenge and embrace these qualities: they manipulate rapidly changing conditions of temporality, contingency, movement, multiplicity, sensation and affect in order to prompt potentialities particular to the landscape medium. Importantly, dioramic modes are intended to be used in tandem with more conventional representation techniques, with the desire to challenge their assumptions and to evoke ephemeral and ever-changing environmental conditions that often evade them.

Many of the qualitative strategies my students and I have developed combine analog construction with photographic documentation. Photography and photomontage are important operations in an iterative process of constructing spatio-material conditions in time.[4] The photographic image indexes real, phenomenal processes in an immediate way that foregrounds manifold temporalities imperative to the landscape design process.[5] The imaging strategies of dioramas incorporate two-dimensional context as spatial extent with models objectifying a foreground condition, integrating both experiential and phenomenal information, the immediate and the distant. My students are exploring dioramic modes in the studio context through analog techniques of incorporating natural and cultural processes through an iterative, feedback method combining photomontage with actual materials in a three-dimensional construction. These constructions test the unique potential for the transformation of representation in the contemporary landscape design processes. Dioramic modes lie at the intersection of perception as a form of knowledge and the necessity to represent changing, natural processes defining the landscape medium.[6]

Typically, we initiate the process by constructing a temporary, three-dimensional, makeshift space/enclosure from cardboard or other pliable materials held together by pins or tape, the aim of which is to facilitate rapid changeability and to destabilize the singular, static, immobile, illusionistic and illustrative character of the conventional diorama. The interior of the construction is lined with photographic or photomontaged images in order to provide scalar context and extent, while also indexing large-scale phenomenal, ephemeral and temporal landscape conditions (climate, ecotone, meteorology, geomorphology, etc.). The images are also temporarily pinned or taped, and derived from the student's own photographic archive, instead of a process of random selection from pre-existing published sources. The surfaces of the enclosure may be warped, gapped, punctured and/or shifted, depending on the initial or subsequent investigation, in order to provide light as aspect to the interior. Movable materials are inserted into the box to induce a creative experience of tactile, olfactory and spatial thinking. It is crucial that the materials sustain a suggestive and scalar ambiguity, rather than a literal reading, in order to generate an openness to multiple, potential creative interpretations. The agency found in deploying phenomenal processes related to a real landscape, such as humidifying, wetting, burning, melting and decomposition, is essential to movement as the instigator of multiple temporalities.

The temporary construction is then itself serially photographed from various angles and under differing ephemeral conditions throughout the exploration in order to record/index the unique qualities of landscape processes. The photographs thus generated reveal unexpected relationships and associations that further inform the exploration. The process folds back on itself as these new photographic images, as well as three-dimensional materials, are then incorporated back into the initial spatio-material construction, promoting reinterpretation, discovery and mobility. Such a rapid and iterative process of experiential exploration can repeat difference indefinitely.[7] The message that we aim to convey to students of landscape architecture and associated fields of design is that it is imperative to halt and challenge the constantly accelerating and ever-upgrading modes of digital representation with an analog process – to provide a counterbalance of physical construction and the sensorial engagement of materials. Experientially severed from the complexities of natural phenomena, a purely digital process can potentially degrade and flatten the ecological dynamism of the landscapes it seeks to represent, be it the stench of a swamp, a subsoil horizon of roots, or the chill of a harbor at dusk. The claim of dioramic modes is not to replace one mode of representation with another, or to create a competition between techniques, but rather to reconcile and diversify multiple modes of landscape representation with the hope that students can begin to develop a personal workflow operating at the intersection of the analog and the digital, the fantastical and the practical, the iterative and the open-ended.

Notes

1 For more on repressed representational techniques that challenge the hegemony of perspectival illusionism, see Jay, M. "Scopic regimes of modernity," in Hal Foster, ed., *Vision and Visuality*. New York: Dia Foundation for Art, 1988, pp. 3–23.

2 See, for example, Oettermen, S. *The Panorama: History of a Mass Medium*. New York: D.L. Schneider, 1997, pp. 69–90; Parcell, S. "The metaphoric architecture of the diorama," *Chora: Intervals in the Philosophy of Architecture*, 2, 1996, pp. 179–216.

3 For a discussion of the agency of the index, see Krauss, R.E. "Notes on the Index: Part 1" and "Notes on the Index: Part 2," in *The Originality of the Avant-Garde and Other Modernist Myths*. Cambridge, MA and London: MIT Press, 1988, pp. 196–219.

4 For the capacity of photography to capture contingency and time, see Doane, M.A. *The Emergence of Cinematic Time: Modernity, Contingency, The Archive*. Cambridge, MA and London: Harvard University Press, 2002.

5 For the potential of the temporary diorama to create ephemeral qualities, see Dezső, S. *Képek/ Photographs 1998–2006*. Budapest: Vintage Galéria, 2007.

6 For the capacity of tactile exploration to generate evocative associations, see Stafford, B. and Terpak, F. *Devices of Wonder*. Los Angeles, CA: Getty Foundation, 2000.

7 The repetition of difference referenced here derives from Gilles Deleuze's thinking, and his interpretation of Nietzche's *élan vital*. See Deleuze, G. *Difference and Repetition*, trans. Paul Patton. New York: Columbia University Press, 1994; Deleuze, G. *Nietzsche and Philosophy*, trans. Hugh Tomlinson. New York: Columbia University Press, 1983.

11.1 a–c

Unseen horizons model and collage strip. The dioramic mode was used to reveal and critically examine the spatial extent of unseen soil mechanics. The theatrical sequence of photographed dioramic manipulations helps to illustrate the accumulation of decaying organic matter and the concurrent formation of the rhizosphere. The illumination of the rhizospheric network corresponds to a theorized increase in fungal symbiont and microfaunal activity. Materials: 2.5-gallon aquarium, water, hot glue, plant roots and stems, tea leaves, felt, sponge pieces, fabric, foam core, micro-beads, glitter, rocks, moss, crushed leaves, collaged photographs, mirror, spray paint, tire shavings, oregano, shredded bird's nest. By Max Hooper Schneider.

11.2 a–b

Swampscape model. Rather than using single-frame photography or reductive digital output, the process of photomontage helped to better define the breadth of textures and density of dead trees among the waterlogged site in question. Previous dioramic experiments helped to achieve the atmospheric scenographs of the site, which were then assembled and montaged together with pictures of collected twigs in Adobe Photoshop. Through many operations of collage and layering, the spatial extent of the dank, swampy environment was established. The production of the final image became exemplary of the hybridization of analog and digital processes of representation. Materials: 2.5-gallon aquarium, water, moss, tea leaves, green acetate, twigs, gravel, thyme, oregano, hot glue, tape, humidifier, desk lamp, flashlight, mirror, collaged photographs, Adobe Photoshop montage, green fabric dye. By Max Hooper Schneider.

11.3 a–c
Rhizosphere: the ecology of neglect – color pencil drawing and collage. These theoretical sections
explore the "ecology of neglect", comparing the robustness of the rhizosphere in a routinely
managed landscape with one that has been abandoned. Such a comparison demonstrates that a
landscape, if left alone, will boost its own biomass, and asserts that all vegetation above-ground is
merely an expression of what is below. A collage-like rendering that combines hand-drawing and
digital media in Adobe Photoshop. By Max Hooper Schneider.

11.4 a–d
Edge-transformation model and collage strip. The two dioramas represent seasonal changes of the proposed meadow/forest edge. Each twig, tied to a yarn thread, is resting loosely on a fur hat. The snowscape is created by layering three jewel cases, each sprayed lightly with baking soda and spread apart to avoid flatness in the photograph. By Leena Cho.

12 Indexing Process
The role of representation in landscape architecture

Andrea Hansen

The issues that concern landscape architects on a daily basis are often fundamentally different from those faced by architects. The obvious factor can be scale when we consider that the scale of landscape may be at times vastly larger than buildings (for instance watersheds and wildlife corridors) and at times far smaller (a planted border or an intimate garden). Time, too, sets us apart in that it is, by necessity, truly woven into the discipline, not only in terms of diurnal programming or as an opportunity for mechanized mobility (as are often the limits of temporality in architecture), but also in consideration of seasonal flux, the maturation of plant material, movement through a site, and the cycles of sun, water, flora and fauna, etc.

Thus, given its unique issues and complexities, why does landscape architecture so often rely on the same representational methods as architecture? The traditional limitation of landscape representation to plans and sections too often has the effect of causing landscape not only to be perceived as flat and superficial, but also in many cases to be designed as such. It is critical that, in this age of concern with the functionality as well as the aesthetics of landscape, we consider the notion of a "thick surface" that considers what is above and below grade, along with the fluctuation of these aspects over time, to be as important as the as-built conditions of the surface itself. Thus landscape architects must begin to explore modes of representation that are palimpsests of time and tectonics, at once visually evocative and hierarchically clear and concise.

The primary challenges of creating such drawings are twofold: first, one must be able to convey a large amount of information, both spatial and data-based, in a way that is sufficiently legible to provide an immediate understanding at first reading, while continuing to reveal more information upon deeper investigation. Second, one must be able to capture a series of temporal and spatial moments in static 2D space since, while compelling and frequently used, video and models still have limitations in concretely describing space.

In my work with students in studio and representation courses at Harvard University Graduate School of Design, an emphasis on informationally complex yet visually clear and compelling drawings has resulted in several drawing types that successfully navigate the aforementioned challenges. The first type might be considered the "sequential series", which juxtaposes a set of "small multiples" (to borrow from infographic guru Edward Tufte) in order to show the progression of an idea, the layers of a design or land form, or the change in certain conditions over time. The series can manifest itself in countless ways, but some good examples are seen in section-elevation series (12.10–12.13), which, in addition to tracking changes in land form across the site, show seasonal change by reflecting foliage cycles as well as the ebb and flow of activity. While Yizhou Xu's series functions temporally, the series employed by Judith Rodriguez (12.5) serves to document the process of transforming a landscape through a series of semi-algorithmic tectonic operations. The second type of drawing is the "measured perspective cut", which employs a variable depth of field or point of view that provides both the depth and strategic angle of a perspective drawing with the rigorous scalability of an orthographic drawing at the cut plane. In a measured perspective cut drawing, the cut plane can be taken parallel to the page, as shown in Figures 12.1 and 12.3–12.5, or at an angle, as demonstrated in Figure 12.9. Regardless, each of these drawings is able to show far more information about the section's tectonic context, both above and below the section line. The final type of drawing is the "indexed infographic", which, unlike the previous two types, removes the constraints of physical space from the drawing to focus instead on comparative or indexical relationships. Comparative relationships are examined in Alexander Arroyo's time-elapse color study of Evans Way Park (12.1), which uses Grasshopper to extract the dominant colors from a series of site photographs taken at timed intervals. Indexical relationships, on the other hand, are demonstrated by Kate Smaby's botanical legend for Evans Way Park (12.6), which acts both as a key to her sections and as a forager's guide that categorizes the types of food or product produced by each species.

Each of these three drawing types – the sequential series, the measured perspective cut and the indexed infographic – layers multiple types of information into one drawing, and often successfully breaks down both ecological and experiential processes and thick 3D space into discrete layers. This is the direction in which landscape architecture must head, because we cannot intervene on the landscape until we fully understand the complexities of the constantly changing world around us. These representational snapshots provide a good survey of the communication styles and media used by students to project their concepts for various landscape types, including productive landscapes, large parks and landscape urbanism.

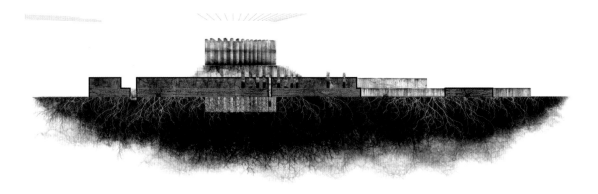

12.1
Fifteen-minute approach to Boston South Station (coming from New York City), de-grading, time-elapse color mapping, using media including interval photography, Photoshop filters, Grasshopper software. By Alexander Arroyo.

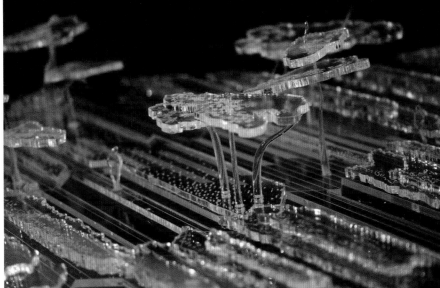

12.2 a–c
Model, hand-drawn textures scanned into illustrator and etched onto acrylic model using laser-cutter. By Senta Burton.

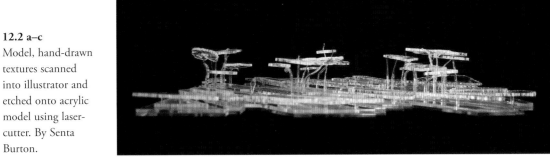

12.3 a–b
Evans Way Park redesign, infiltration, detail plan and detail section, using AutoCAD plan and section line plus
hand-drawn perspective sketches with Photoshop collage, color and texture. By Michael Easler.

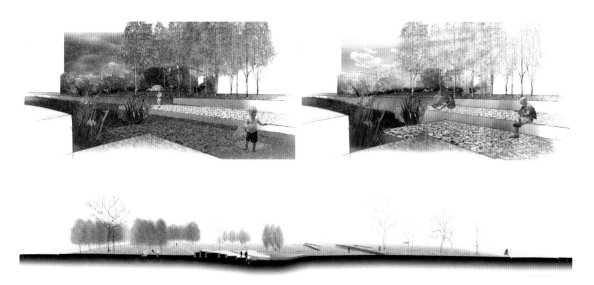

12.4
Evans Way Park redesign, infiltration, long section perspective and perspective views, AutoCAD section line plus hand-drawn perspective sketches with Photoshop collage, color and texture. By Michael Easler.

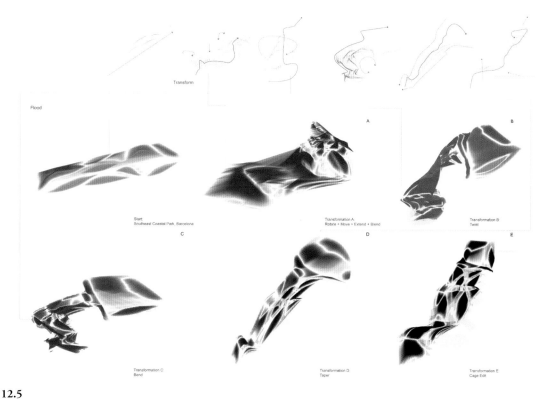

12.5
Floodscapes, site diagram, sectional perspective and montage, using Rhino (for modeling and contour generation), Illustrator and Photoshop. By Judith Rodriguez.

12.6
Botanical legend, section, hand-drawing, watercolor and gouache. By Kate Smaby.

12.7
Acqua Alta, montage, using Rhino (modeling and contour generation), Illustrator and Photoshop. By Irene Toselli.

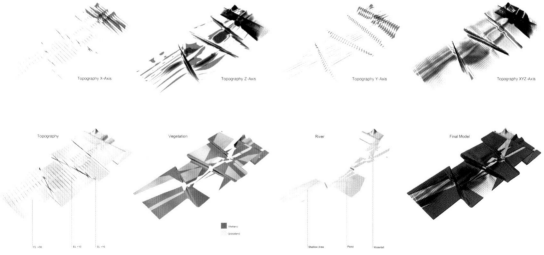

12.8 and 12.9
Fragmented landscapes, site diagram, sectional perspective and montage using Rhino (modeling and section generation),
Illustrator and Photoshop. By Patchara Wongboonsin.

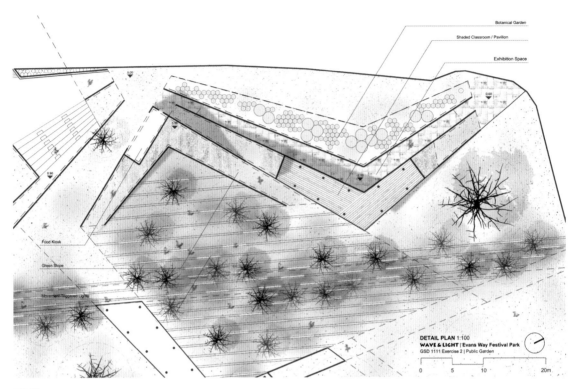

12.10
Wave and light: Evans Way Park, detail plan, AutoCAD, Illustrator and Photoshop. By Yizhou Xu.

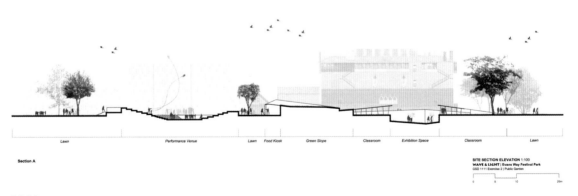

12.11
Wave and light: Evans Way Park, long section, AutoCAD, Illustrator and Photoshop. By Yizhou Xu.

12.12
Wave and light: Evans Way Park, perspective, model photo and Photoshop. By Yizhou Xu.

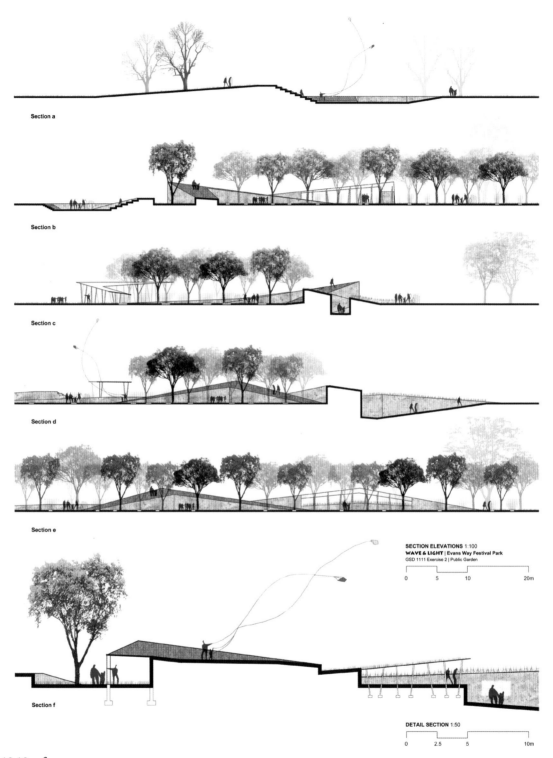

Section a

Section b

Section c

Section d

Section e

SECTION ELEVATIONS 1:100
WAVE & LIGHT | Evans Way Festival Park
GSD 1111 Exercise 2 | Public Garden

0   5   10   20m

Section f

DETAIL SECTION 1:50

0   2.5   5   10m

12.13 a–f
Wave and light: Evans Way Park, section elevation, AutoCAD, Illustrator and Photoshop. By Yizhou Xu.

13 Landscape as Digital Media

David Syn Chee Mah

The following landscape representational works are produced by graduate students within Digital Media, Computational Fluid Dynamics and Digital Fabrication at the Harvard Graduate School of Design. These representational works are driven by the general ambition to promote various digital design, simulation and fabrication tools that are now becoming more accessible to the profession and discipline. The courses and workshops are structured to allow students to actively engage and develop specific techniques and sensibilities through the use of these emerging tools so that their abilities to develop the representational potentials, as well as design and constructive capabilities, of digital media is widened.

Students on these courses have actively developed techniques in the description and generation of intricate landscape organizations and morphologies that have often been elusive to designers due to their complexity. Complex part-to-whole relationships and field organizations that resonate with natural landscape qualities and conditions are made more accessible to designers through digital media. While these media allow them to illustrate and analyze existing landscape organizations and forms, students have also been encouraged to translate these associative techniques to develop landscape design techniques and sensibilities that are equally generative for the design process. Many of the students' projects take advantage of the associative geometric capabilities of digital media to develop various landscape projects that showcase and express innovative design and tectonic sensibilities ranging from the production of a new series of landscape infra-structural types to the specific texture and surface design of a landscape water sculpture proposal. The investigation into associative design techniques also gives students the ability to tie the generation of landscape designs to various influential factors, ranging from specific climatic factors to topographic conditions.

The digital media for landscape representation provide the capability to actively represent landscape processes that operate in time. These include qualities and processes that have traditionally been excessively intricate to convey through visual media. Some of the projects developed at the Harvard Graduate School of Design have used compu-tational fluid dynamics to represent landscape qualities and processes that point towards a performance as well as time-based reading of the consequences and influencing parameters for landscape design. The simulation of hydrodynamics and various processes such as deposition and scour (sedimentation and erosion) as well as water velocity and tidal fluctuation is used by these students to describe the effect of landscape morphology on hydrodynamic processes; conversely, it is also able to simulate the landscape processes already shaping and active on the site.

Extending digital media to construction and fabrication, students in the Fabricating Grounds elective course were charged with developing a series of digitally fabricated models and prototypes, informed by a parallel exercise in utilizing digital media, to geometrically describe complex landscape topographies and surfaces. These geometric exercises were extended into a series of techniques for utilizing landscape representational systems as modalities for assembling and fabricating various landscape models and prototypes. The course allowed students to establish relationships between the protocols for representation and description with a system of generation and production.

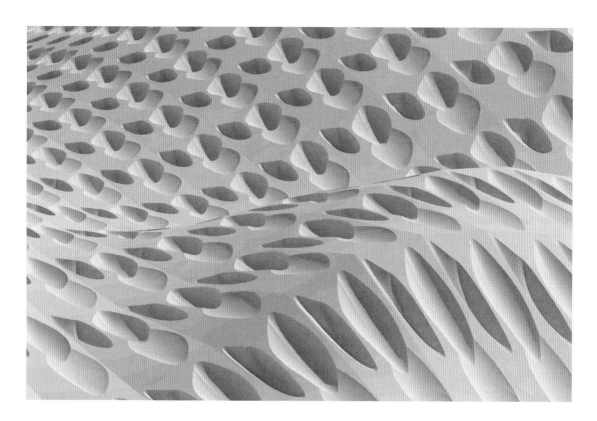

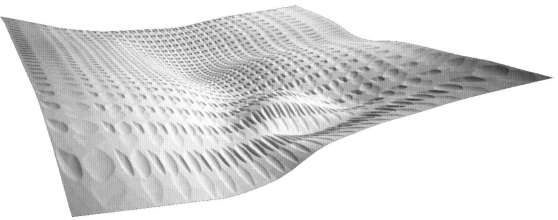

13.1 a–b
Splash block surface texture design, using Rhinoceros, Grasshopper and Rhinoscript. By Ilana Cohen.

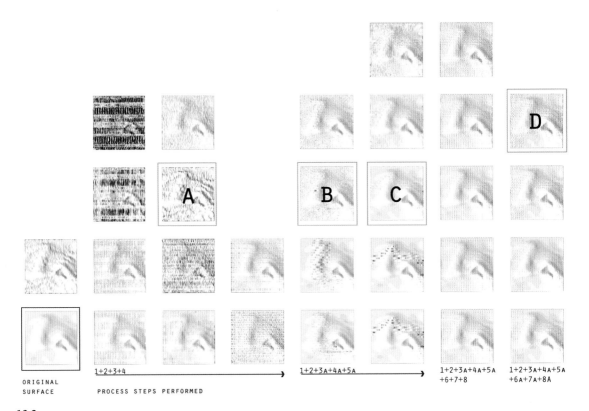

13.2
Texture coding and generation process diagram, using Rhinoceros, Grasshopper and Rhinoscript. By Ilana Cohen.

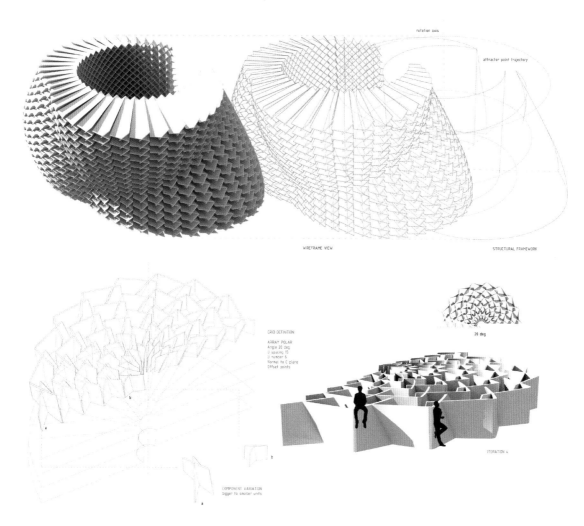

13.3
Garden pavilion design and tectonic development, using Rhinoceros and Grasshopper. By Sandra Herrera.

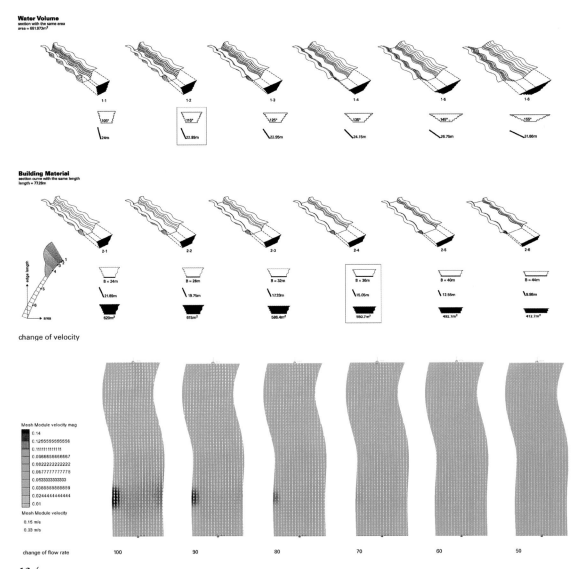

13.4
Catalog of hydrological infrastructural types generated by associative design and hydrodynamic simulation depicting dynamic infrastructure, using Rhinoceros, Aquaveo CMS Flow and Grasshopper. By Xinpeng Yu.

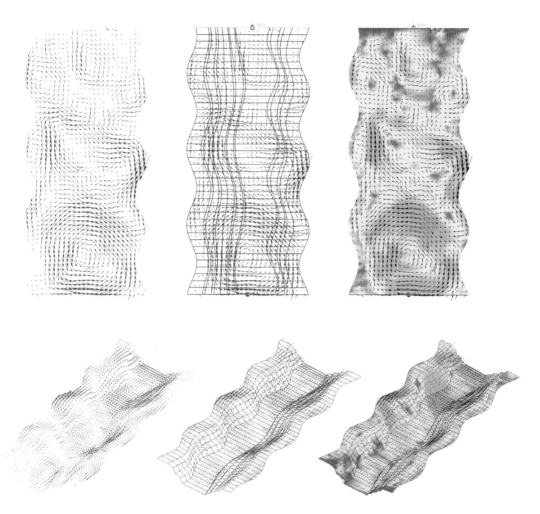

13.5 a–f
Hydrodynamic simulation of channel prototype depicting dynamic infrastructure, using Rhinoceros, Aquaveo CMS Flow and Grasshopper. By Xinpeng Yu.

13.6
Garden design fabricated model (digitally fabricated model for Fabricating Grounds). By Lisl Kotheimer and Marcus Owens.

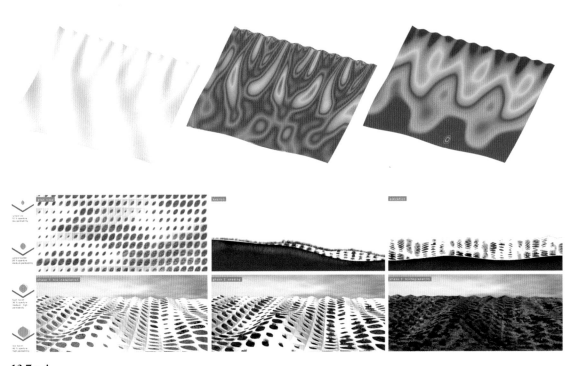

13.7 a–i
Surface analysis and differentiated ground-tilling system and projected transformation (for Fabricating Grounds), using software including Rhinoceros, Grasshopper and Rhinoterrain. By Forbes Lipschitz.

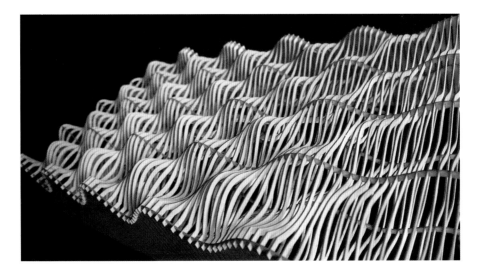

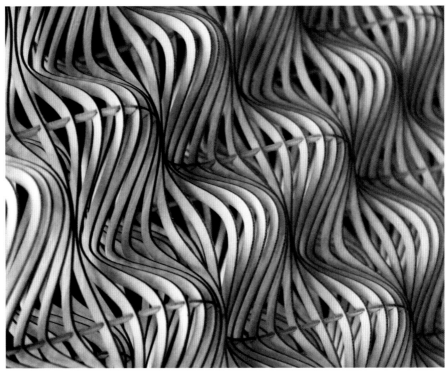

13.8 a–b
Surface description/ moiré effect, fabricated (for Fabricating Grounds) using software including Rhinoceros, Grasshopper. By Alpa Nawre and Jing Zhang.

14 Mat Ecologies
Landscape representations

Chris Reed

The mat can be thought of as a systematic field of consistent and repetitive parts, dispersed across a large-scale territory, and governed by a set of formal or logistical operations. The mat is transformed according to its own internal logics, or in response to external inputs, or both; in architecture and urbanism, for example, the mat may transform in response to how it hits the ground, or to what programmatic desires are brought to bear, while simultaneously retaining its identity.

Yet the potential of the mat lies in its transformative effects through time – its ability to catalyse and provoke a set of emergent and provisional dynamics and relationships, ecologies and economies. The mat stages open-ended futures: it sets up conditions for use and appropriation in its delineation; it offers itself for opportunistic appropriation; and it is capable of responding to input through a set of unfolding operational principles. Thus mats have agency; they catalyse transformation; they form and perform across regional, metropolitan fields yet are able to morph in response to localized inputs.

In this way, mats act much like engineering technologies and systems, which are themselves characterized by a set of component parts or units, governed by operational logics, that can be deployed flexibly across sites or territories in ways that respond to conditions on the ground – yet without giving up their signifying characteristics.

The mat ecologies studio (with Harvard Graduate School of Design and the University of Toronto's Faculty of Architecture, Landscape, and Design) focused on these potential linkages – on the way in which program and performance could inform mat strategies for large-scale metropolitan landscapes. In this case, we were interested primarily in remediation technologies, and their social, ecological, cultural and urbanistic potentials. And we focused on their deployment on a large military reservation in eastern Massachusetts which was recently subject to mission realignment – Massachusetts Military Reservation, Cape Cod, USA.

The central question for the studio is this: What is the generative potential of this vast deindustrialized and demilitarized landscape, and of the remedial technologies that may be deployed in its reclamation and recovery? How do we grapple with residual, defunct landscapes and their physical (contamination), perceptual (image), and economic challenges? Newer economies of production, lifestyle, leisure or tourism cannot possibly address them in total, at least at first; there is simply too much land, too few resources, and often too much time. At a time in which both production and urbanism are being radically reconsidered, how might productive seeds be planted to generate, through time, a new set of urbanistic practices, founded upon and grounded in the degenerated military–industrial landscape? How might these strategies incorporate both the dynamics and latencies of industrialization and militarization, of post-industrial hibernation, and of potential shifts in military roles and responsibilities to forge new ecologies of use and disuse?

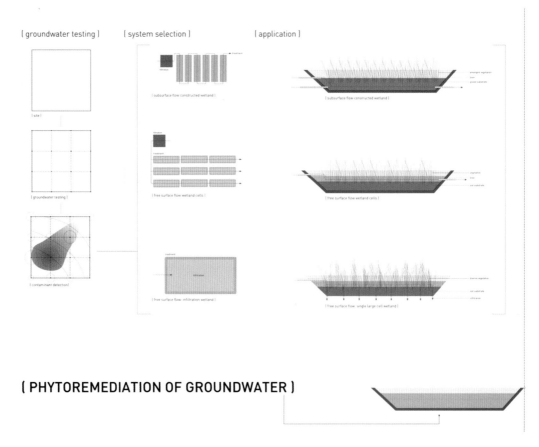

[groundwater testing]   [system selection]   [application]

(PHYTOREMEDIATION OF GROUNDWATER)

14.1

Mat units and logics: groundwater remediation and desert navigation training. Drawings outline the components of remediation and training systems – and their operational logics – for possible deployment across the site. Deployments are flexible, but they (and their constituent units) must behave according to the rules outlined herein. AutoCAD base, with Adobe Suite. By Geneva Wirth (Harvard Graduate School of Design; project title: Disturbance Ecologies).

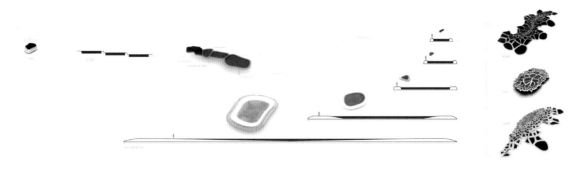

14.2

Groundwater remediation units and assemblies. Rhino, Rhino scripting, 3ds Max, V-Ray, Adobe Suite. By Geneva Wirth.

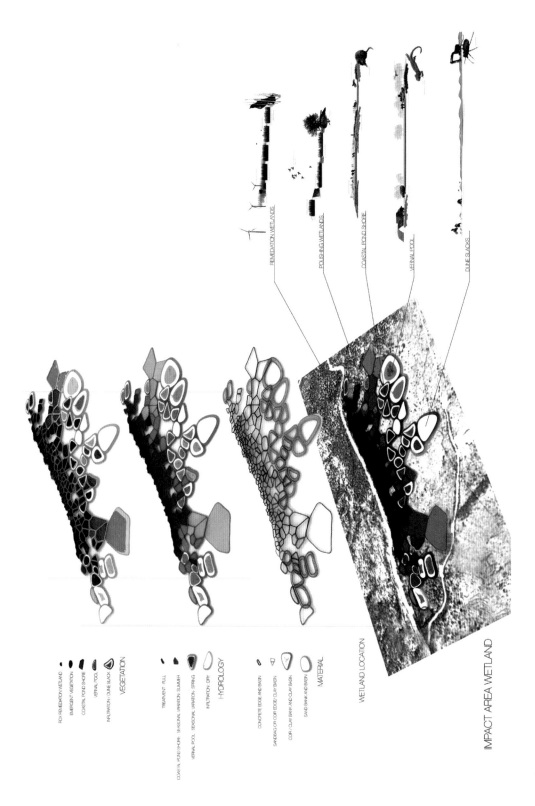

14.3

Groundwater remediation mat deployment, with systems and demonstrations. Rhino, Rhino scripting, 3ds Max, V-Ray, Adobe Suite. By Geneva Wirth.

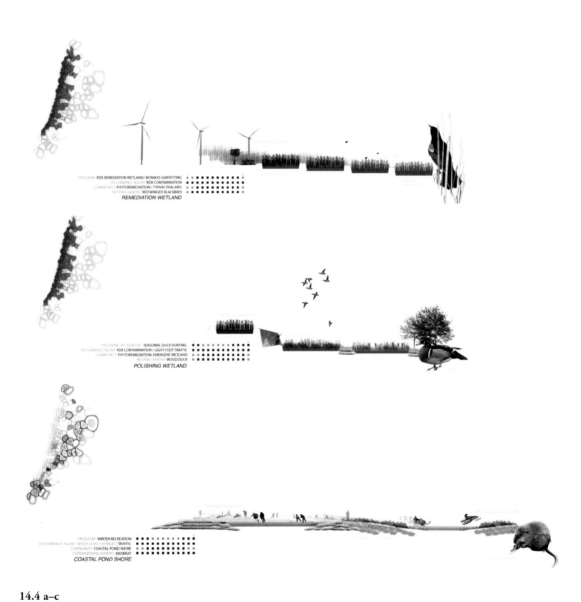

14.4 a–c
Groundwater remediation demonstrations, showing physical and programmatic variations. Rhino, Rhino scripting, 3ds Max, V-Ray, Adobe Suite. By Geneva Wirth.

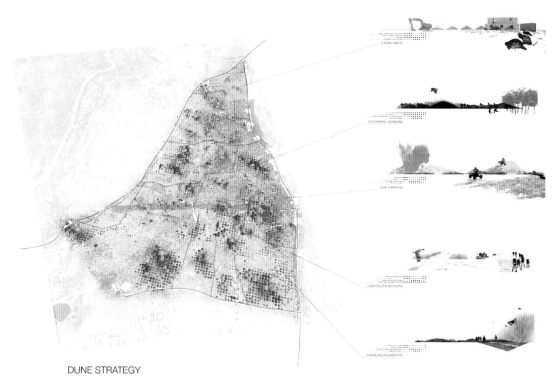

DUNE STRATEGY

14.5
Desert navigation training mat deployment, with systems and demonstrations. Rhino, Rhino scripting, 3ds Max, V-Ray, Adobe Suite. By Geneva Wirth.

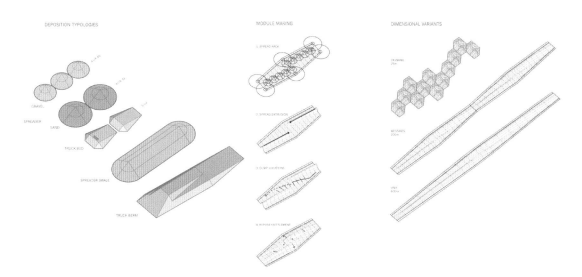

14.6 a–c
Soil deposition and stockpiling strategies, depicting typologies and variants. Rhino, 3ds Max, Adobe Suite. By Kelly Nelson Doran (University of Toronto; project title: Fixing Forces.)

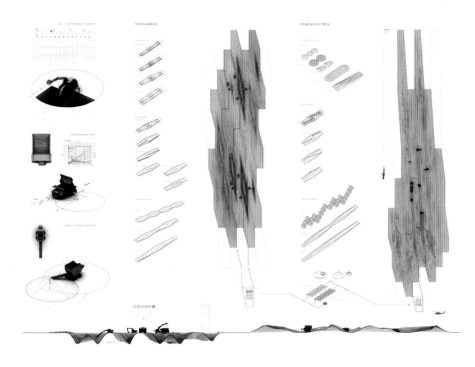

14.7
Techniques
and assemblies
depicting the tools
and aggregated
assemblies of
trenching and
stockpiling
strategies. Rhino,
3ds Max, Adobe
Suite. By Kelly
Nelson Doran.

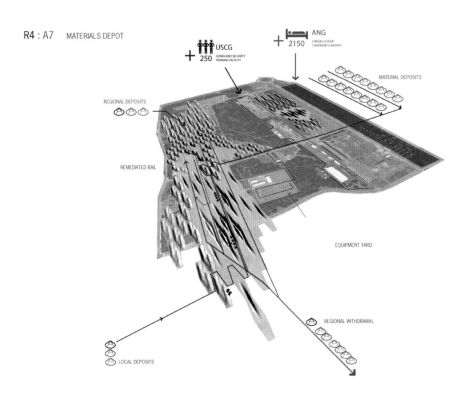

14.8
Deployment: the
materials depot.
Demonstration
of physical and
operational
deployment of
the mat, and the
various relationships
established between
soil-washing
operations,
personnel
deployments, base
economies and site
logistics. Rhino, 3ds
Max, Adobe Suite.
By Kelly Nelson
Doran.

14.9 a–b

Image of roadside, grain silos, perspective – collage, digitally composed. The bounty of grain in surplus and production at a rhythm of towns at every twenty or so miles along the logistical railway. These constellations of vertical landmarks are often the only architecture in a sea of horizontal landscape. These views show an overlay that indexes the existence and various conditions or levels of the Ogallala Aquifer on an existing and acknowledged infrastructure. By Erik Prince (Harvard Graduate School of Design; design thesis, Master's in Landscape Architecture 2.)

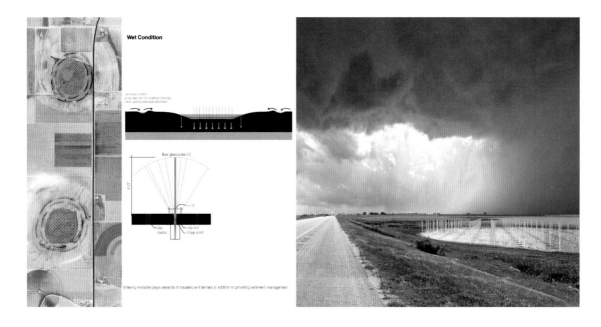

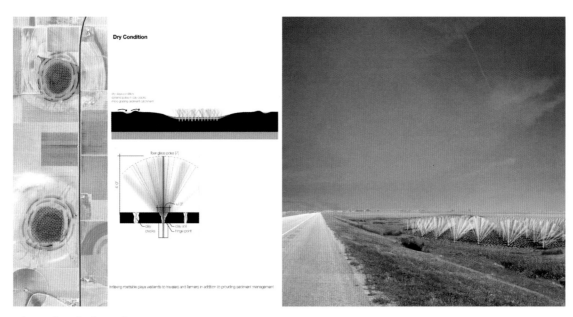

14.10 a–b and 14.11 a–b

Plan, section, perspective, mixed media, collage, illustrated section, aerial overlay, representing playa wetlands index – wet condition.14.10, indexing roadside playa wetlands, which are ephemeral shallow basins that are often farmed over and are important moments of aquifer recharge. This view shows dynamics of the proposed basin shortly after a rain storm. 14.11, depicting dry conditions: this view shows dynamics of the proposed basin during the vast stretches of time when the basins do not contain water. By Erik Prince.

Escarpment and plateau of the High Plains

14.12 a–h
Diagram section
and roadside
sequence of views
using mixed media,
illustrated section,
photographs,
photo collage. The
sequence of entering
the Ogallala Aquifer
region involves
an accent up the
escarpment where
layered roadside
planting inscribes
a contrasting
experience upon
entering a vast, flat
and treeless plain of
the region. By Erik
Prince.

Diagram section for the Entrance Rumble / Layered roadside planting

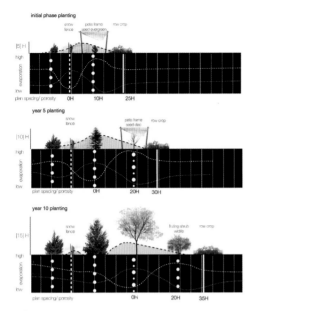
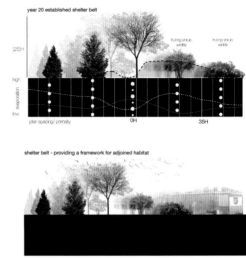

14.13 a–e

Section diagrams over time, mixed media (collage section) drawing depicting water-level change shelter-belt planting. A section diagram establishing the shelter belts over time using ideal spacing, micro-climatic wind, sun/shade and precipitation manipulations. By Erik Prince.

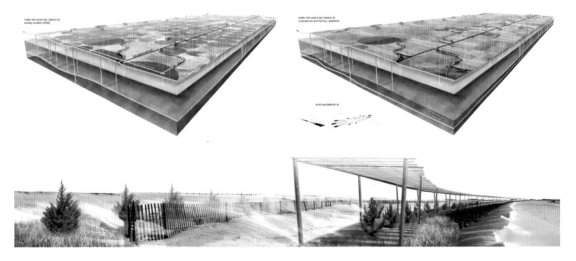

14.14 a–c

Aerial section and perspective, mixed media, digital model and Photoshop image modification, depictions of "water-level change shelter-belt axons". A series of drawings that draw on the shelter-belt layout and its relationship to the aquifer and land use over time. Dynamics of the wind and the corresponding landscape framework that provides resiliency, a visual translation of the land use, and a backbone for ecological habitat. By Erik Prince.

14.15
Landscape
perspective, collage,
mixed media,
Photoshop image
modification
depicting crossroad
garden perspective of
the dynamics of the
Sandhills landscape.
The design induces
disturbance (grazing,
fire and wind)
dynamics, creating
dune landscape
and topographic
variation to heighten
aquifer-recharge
potential, ecological
diversity and a
focused microcosm
experience of the
greater landscape. By
Erik Prince.

14.16 a–b
Aerial section and
diagram section,
mixed-media collage,
depicting an aerial-
axonometric view
of the Sandhills
crossroad garden
that shows the
relationship of the
design-induced
dynamics to the
context (surface and
subsurface) and to
the topography and
program. By Erik
Prince.

15 Exploration Drawings Mixed Media

Bradley Cantrell and Jeff Carney

Before embarking on an exploration of the Rio Grande Valley, a tool was developed to serve as a device for reading and surveying the landscape. It needed to be simple and easily portable, while also providing a medium by which the landscape could be measured. The chosen tool was a pair of collapsible poles built from durable PVC pipe. The poles were each 12 feet tall and 3 inches thick, painted bright red for visibility and marked every 3 feet for height reference.

As the team moved throughout the border zone, the poles were positioned and photographed to highlight important aspects of each site. The tool evolved with the exploration process, and the versatility of the poles allowed for site-specific analysis and measurement. At each site, the poles were photographed in different positions to describe aspects such as elevation change, water usage, scale, vegetation patterns, terrain formation and human movement.

When returning from the border expedition, the photographs were pieced together and analyzed further. Two additional layers of information were added: a layer of linework to emphasize what the poles highlighted, and a layer of labels to represent sounds, smells, feelings and sights that the group observed while on the site. After analyzing the photographs, a rendered section of the space between the poles was created. The final renderings put the viewer into the site, allowing a glimpse into the experience of each place.

Over a few days, we worked together to devise a piece of equipment or tool to survey the landscape as we pass through it. This tool is more than a device for collection, it is an object that engages with the environment, allowing us to understand how the environment becomes a landscape through our knowing it.

We all know that it takes a lifetime to truly "understand" a place. We know our hometown in a way we will never know anyplace else. The fabric of our environment shapes us while we simultaneously formulate our understanding of it. To truly understand the condition of the "local" is to be completely immersed in it and see it through many different lenses. Can we understand even the basic structure of a complex culture in a few days of visiting? Will we be able to comprehend the function of an ecosystem that we are unfamiliar with?

The following images are extracted from our studio and advanced digital media courses at Louisiana State University. A variety of image selections depict poetic and expressive collages/digital photomontages, sketch models, hybrid drawing section elevations, landscapes composed using virtually all digital media means (including 3ds Max) and collage methods to depict program events and system changes.

15.1 a–c
Sections – traditional and digital media, photomontage, hybrid drawing, Rio Grande Kayak
Park. By John Oliver.

15.2 a–c
Perspective –
photomontage of
Rio Grande Kayak
Park, depicting
various site
conditions. Balance
of dark hues with
highlighted spaces
for emphasis.
Atmospheric
applications
add a realistic
appeal to these
photomontages. By
John Oliver.

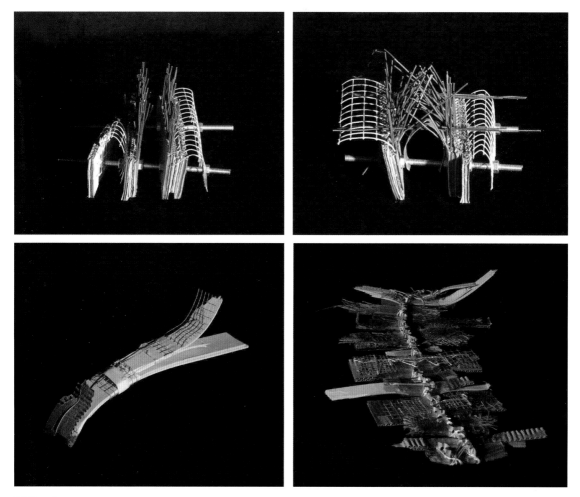

15.3 a–d
Sketch models – cardboard, metal, wood, Rio Grande Kayak Park trail. By John Oliver.

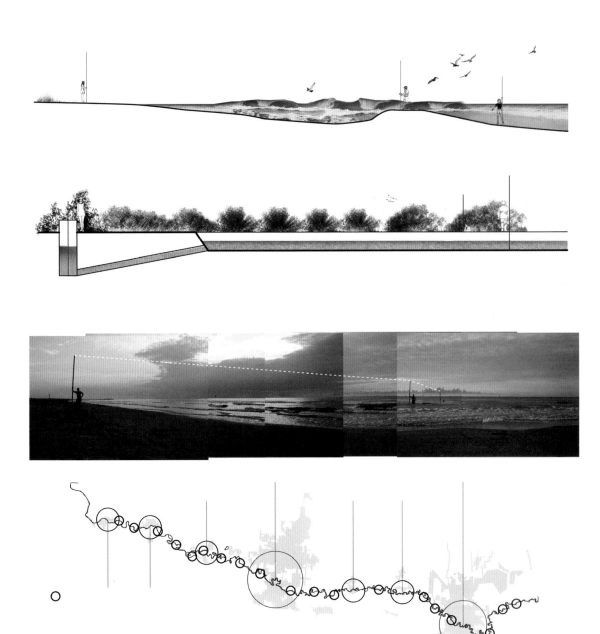

15.4 a–d
Through your eyes – section pieces of the sandbar CAD and Photoshop collage. By Will Benge, John Oliver and Kelly Sprinkle.

15.5
Shelter array composite using 3ds Max, rendered using V-Ray, photo altered in Photoshop. By Joaquin Martinez.

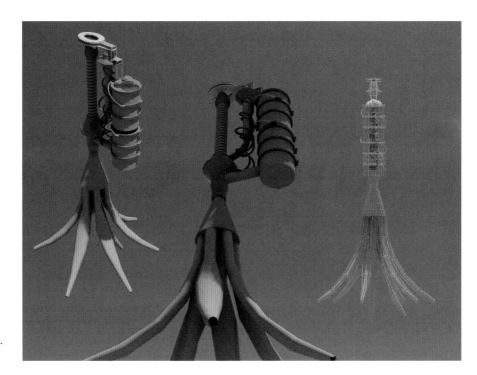

15.6
Geothermal heat pump using 3ds Max and Photoshop. By Natalie Yates.

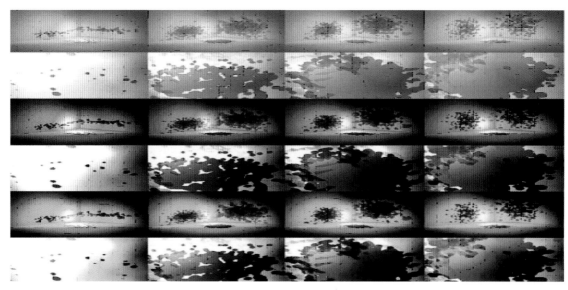

15.7
Particle flow diagrams, fields of perception using 3ds Max. By Natalie Yates.

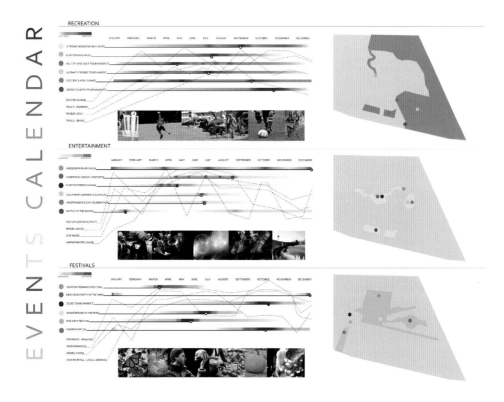

15.8
Drawing showing events calendar and program strategy development for the park. By A. Baum, M. Ellender, C. LeBeau, K. Lonon, P. May, P. McGannon, S. Miller, B. Moran, A. Ramirez and C. Thonn.

TRAIL SYSTEM BREAKDOWN

the trail system that travels throughout the park is established according to type, creating a hierarchy based on use. There are three main levels: hiking, cycling, and mountain biking. Capacity meters are placed along certain entry points to allow for user monitoring.

15.9 a–f
Trail system analysis for the park. By A. Baum, M. Ellender, C. LeBeau, K. Lonon, P. May, P. McGannon, S. Miller, B. Moran, A. Ramirez and C. Thonn.

SEASONAL CHANGE IN MATERIALS

LOWLANDS
- *Solidago nutans* (Indian Grass)
- *Echinacea purpurea* (Purple Coneflower)

MIDLANDS
- *Taxodium distichum* (Bald Cypress)
- *Acer rubrum var. drummondii* (Swamp Red Maple)

UPLANDS
- *Pinus Palustris* (Longleaf Pine)
- *Magnolia grandiflora* (Southern Magnolia)

AXIS PLANTING
- *Liriodendron tulipifera* (Tulip Tree)
- *Carya illinoinensis* (Pecan Tree)

CONSISTENT MATERIALS

15.10 a–c
Complementary materials palette for the park. By A. Baum, M. Ellender, C. LeBeau, K. Lonon, P. May, P. McGannon, S. Miller, B. Moran, A. Ramirez and C. Thonn.

- Basin Model
- Grass Vegetation Ground Cover
- Gravel Variety Ground Cover
- Large Glass Openings

LIFE CYCLE CHANGE IN MATERIALS

- Concrete Panel Architectural Structures
- Redwood Structures & Screens
- Corten Steel

16 Hybrid Drawings

Mikyoung Kim

Drawings are the engine for knowledge in design. They move us closer to an understanding of spatial experience and materiality. In the past decade, for better or worse, digital media have taken over the realm of two-dimensional communication in the field of landscape architecture. The software tools utilized are effective in their approximation of reality, but often homogenize the unique character of the individual voice. This observation became the seed for a research project through a series of seminars at Rhode Island School of Design (RISD) over the past eight years, looking at drawings that are hybridized conditions between manual and digital representation. Multiple technologies of drawing, including photography, scanning, collage, Xeroxing, bricolage, Photoshop, SketchUp, AutoCAD, the laser cutter, Rhino, charcoal, pencil, ball-point pens, ink, pastel, dirt, acrylic and oil paints, asphalt, resin, wax and other materials, and software programs, were the basis of experimentation in two-dimensional communication. Last year, this research project culminated with an advanced seminar co-taught with Scott Carman, who taught the digital component. The drawings shown here are a representation of drawings that blur the boundaries between digital and analog systems with RISD students in landscape architecture, architecture and interior architecture.

The ground

From that study, students explored various "ground" materials to develop their work. They experimented with a wide range of materials, including stone, wood, particle board, canvas, fabric, acetate, plastic, resin, and various store-bought and handmade papers. The idea was to find a way in which the pigments and materials applied on the surface could have a dialog that moved past the conventional ink-to-paper relationship. Ground surfaces defined the typology of interface and the tools allowed for the drawing. Students who worked with heartier and denser materials were able to expand their utensils to include more aggressive drawing mechanisms such as torches of various sizes, knives, and the laser cutter set at various speeds. Poured materials, such as plaster and resin, had a more fluid process where the ground material often acted as the surface and texture for elements in the drawing. Carving became part of the vocabulary of drawing with these constructed fluid grounds. Students explored textures and ways in which drawing devices interacted with surficial allowances. Roughly textured surfaces had a muscular reaction to the tools, resisting the material at certain points and absorbing them at others. This study allowed students to see beyond the conventions of paper to an expansion of the dialog between surface and line.

The engine

The instruments were considered from a wide range of options – pencils, charcoal, ink, gouache, erasers, white-out, pens, markers, watercolors, tape, dirt, asphalt, knives, torches, laser cutters, laser printers, Xerox machines, resin, wood and fabric. Software tools included Photoshop, Illustrator, AutoCAD, Rhino, 3ds Max and SketchUp. The engine was the device that transformed the ground surface. Students worked through an iterative process to develop innovative ways of studying concepts with appropriate materials. An important component of the research was to discover interfaces between manual and digital tools for drawing, and finding a hybrid between the two. Techniques included the layering of multiple processes and utilizing the scanner and copying machine as a way of overlapping a rich set of drawing typologies. Printing techniques included oversaturating papers or lightly printing layers of images. Digital and manual collage and bricolage was a common theme in merging the two technologies. The projects looked at a thesis of how drawings can be immersed into the process of design at all the phases of work, from concept sketches to detailing drawing with specific materiality. This rich layering of materials offered students a venue to create a set of drawings that operate not only as an individual expression of their vision, but also as communication tools that convey information about the scale, tenor and materiality of proposed work.

In the end, the goal was to be able to create drawings that were unique and individual to the site, the project's concerns, and the student's evolving vision. Work was developed beyond illustrative representation of a fixed idea to one where process and experience were captured through the drawings. The search, over these collaborative studies, was to develop an understanding of the analog and digital tools available to us as landscape architects and the way in which they can blur to create a new typology of drawing that is both and neither.

16.1
Perspective. Sepia tone. Mixed media and technique from Photoshop, Rhino, photography, charcoal, ink, eraser, glue, Xeroxing, scanning, charcoal drawing and digital collage. By Stephen Comstock.

16.2

Perspective. Mixed media and technique, gouache, graphite, watercolor, elements and landscape and architectural features digitally collaged in Photoshop, using Rhinoceros model as base. By Shushmita Mizan.

16.3
Axonometric. Mixed media and technique, gouache, graphite, watercolor, elements and landscape and architectural features digitally collaged in Photoshop using Rhinoceros model as base. By Shushmita Mizan.

16.4 a–b

Perspective drawings. Charcoal and ink drawing on textured paper, vertical orientation, application of light and dark contrasting shades and shadow create dramatic scene. By Sean Henderson.

16.5
Perspective drawing. Charcoal, white Conté crayon and ink drawing on textured paper, horizontal orientation, application of light and dark contrasting shades and shadow create dramatic scene. Strips of light and shaded areas leading to vanishing point create depth and dramatic feel. By Prakkamakul Ponnapa.

16.6
Collage perspective. Watercolor, graphite and elements digitally collaged into scene. Horizontal orientation creates strong panoramic scene. Landscape elements bleeding off white frame space of drawing, giving a "looseness" to the overall quality of the drawing. By Prakkamakul Ponnapa.

16.7
Perspective.
Charcoal, ink,
graphite, Photoshop
and collaged
drawing with
strong contrasting
chiaroscuro effects.
Sharp lines leading
to a clear vanishing
point create a
strong perspective
with spatial depth.
By Prakkamakul
Ponnapa.

16.8
Perspective. Sepia
tone. Mixed media
and technique
from photography,
Xeroxing, scanning,
graphite drawing
and digital collage.
By Laurencia
Strauss.

16.9
Collage perspective.
Photography,
charcoal, pastel,
ink, graphite, and
Photoshop. By
Filomena Riganti.

16.10
Collage perspective.
Photoshop and
SketchUp with
watercolor, pastel
and graphite. By
Filomena Riganti.

16.11
Perspective.
Photoshop, drawing
with charcoal,
ink and eraser. By
Eduardo Terranova.

16.12 a–d
Collage perspective. Xerox, photography, Photoshop with gouache, pastel and graphite. By Damian Augsberger.

16.13
Perspective. Photoshopped photograph with graphite and charcoal drawing, loose sketch with delicate shade and shadow effects. By Bo Young Seo.

17 From Fabrics and Diagrams to Scenarios

Stephen Luoni

An important function of the University of Arkansas Community Design Center (UACDC) involves preparation of interested upper-year architecture and landscape architecture students for leadership roles in the creative development of the built environment. This initiates questions on the dynamics of speculative practice and "critical practitioner" thinking. Design entails practitioner agency within a discursive field of socio-environmental issues beyond traditional skills in form making. More than simply an illustration or pictorial description, drawing as a logic is fundamental in developing projective thinking, from the framing, mapping and analysis of complex issues, to the crafting of design approaches and their communication with the public. At UACDC, information is developed and managed through various drawing logics – fabrics, diagrams and scenario plans – that engage problems of "context production" or the making of place. As an outreach center of the Fay Jones School of Architecture, UACDC fosters design methodologies and visual communications applicable to community development issues.

Jane Jacobs states that the city and other forms of human settlement entail "problems in organized complexity"[1]. Everything, and every design problem, is a landscape regardless of the discipline or scale from which one begins. While students are typically asked to work from the abstract to the concrete in formulating a design framework, crafting a spatial and experiential dimension in place making is always the goal. Four learning objectives define UACDC studios and the roles of drawing in each objective.

- First, introduce students to pressing socio-environmental conditions for which design has a unique capacity to deliver integrated solutions. Students are challenged with contemporary design problems in low-impact development infrastructure, suburban retrofitting, public space and neighborhood revitalization, affordable housing, urban watershed planning, and context-sensitive highway design solutions. Drawings become the argument for certain drivers of growth; diagrams can become the program growth around underutilized local assets; and site plans, for example, communicate subsequent design development.

- Second, engage students in multiple decision-making aspects through allied knowledge fields and multidisciplinary practices as they author design proposals. Urban design and landscape urbanism engage the human experience across multiple properties, scales and private/public realms in shaping the built environment. Their principles of integration are tied to design vocabularies that address interactivity, timing, phasing and connectivity, and should not be confused with principles of composition.

- Third, introduce analysis of precedents and design methods into the design process as research to leverage design intelligence. Analytic drawings are opportunities to formulate vocabularies of looking and making. Fabric diagrams initiate an understanding of the morphology of various town patterns and their capacity, or lack thereof, to create memorable environments. Patterns that are the outcome of various forces or typological conditions – town squares, campuses, parks, grids, edges, corridors, edges, hillsides, etc. – are studied in terms of their grain, scale, geometry and activity. Activity diagrams map explicit and latent user activities as an order or network logic, particularly useful in diffused landscapes where geometric descriptions would prove inadequate.

- Fourth, establish an outreach ethic in which information, arguments and design proposals are visualized intelligently so that they communicate effectively with lay audiences. In these ways, drawing avoids the occupational hazard of designers communicating primarily with other designers. Perspectives are developed in a painterly tradition that makes ideas available to general perception. Proposed spaces are imagined through craftsmanship in pictorial depth, scale, light, texture, proportion, mood and floristic effects to distill a critical thesis beyond simple portraiture or vignette.

Envisioning future development projections is a critical role held by the designer, and the ability to use the power of drawing as a deep, discursive tool to participate in the shaping of public sentiment and policy of this kind is paramount. In public interest design, drawing needs to illuminate and inspire, rather than mystify.

Note

1   Jacobs, J. *The Death and Life of Great American Cities*. New York: Routledge, 1961.

17.1
2030 scenario plan for Fayetteville Eco-City. Digitally generated axonometric showcasing new growth patterns using riparian corridors and ecologically based stormwater management as the armature for new urban development. 3D model generated in 3ds Max. Google Earth underlay and landscape elements are added in Adobe Photoshop. By Graham Patterson.

17.2

Landscape as medium. Matrix of diagrams. In the effort to quickly familiarize architecture students with formal principles in ecological design, photos of landscapes were analyzed for their latent order or moment of coherence. Hand-drawn sketches scanned and manipulated using Adobe Illustrator's Live Trace command. By Eric Dempsey, Courtney Gunderson, Kelly Spearman, Lee Stewart, Christopher Sullivan and Lori Yazwinski.

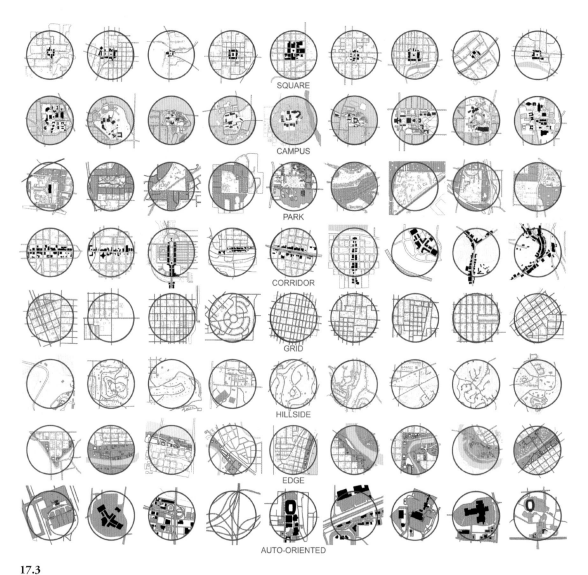

17.3

Arkansas fabrics. Diagrams. Students examined and catalogued scale, grain, geometry and arrangement of traditional town patterns within a half-mile pedestrian shed. Google Earth images scaled and traced in AutoCAD and exported to Adobe Illustrator to manipulate shades and line weights. By Cory Amos, Joshua Clemence, Jimmy Coldiron, Benjamin Curtin, Andrew Darling, Elsa Pandozi, Brian Poepsel, Michela Sgalambro and Lauren Vogl.

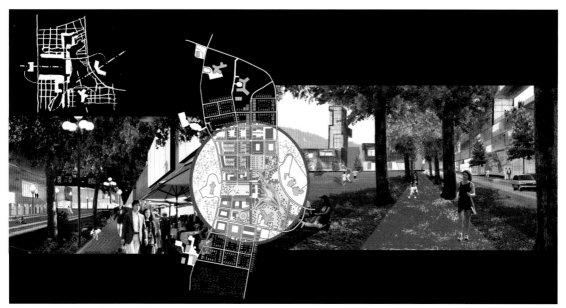

17.4

Cities without cities: a new town center for Bella Vista. Studies of a high-density, mixed-use town center developed around a series of public greens that negotiate hillside terrain. Architectural elements in each perspective are hand-drawn and watercolored. Surface materials, landscape elements and images of people superimposed onto watercolor in Adobe Photoshop. Plan drawing generated in AutoCAD and later exported to Adobe Illustrator for shade and line weight modifications. By Benjamin Curtin.

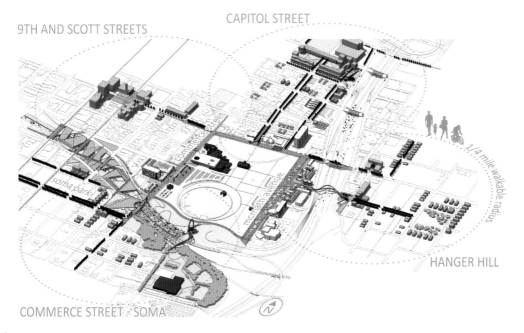

17.5

MacArthur Park District Master Plan, Little Rock. Axonometric of an urban park used as an anchor to re-stitch four adjacent neighborhoods. 3D model generated in Google SketchUp and exported to Adobe Illustrator to manipulate colors and line weights. By Tim Schmidt.

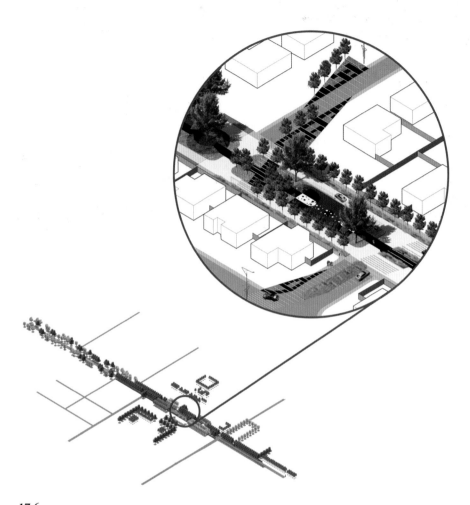

17.6

Highways to greenways, Springdale. Axonometric drawing depicting a retrofitted arterial
road that stitches suburban developments through intensification of the surface with graphic
landscapes complemented by low-impact development technologies and tree-lined rooms. 3D
model generated in AutoCAD and exported to Adobe Illustrator to manipulate colors and line
weights. Landscape elements, pedestrians and cars are overlaid in Adobe Photoshop. By Cory
Amos.

17.7
Parking lot as a natural stormwater treatment system. Digital crafted perspective depicts a retrofit of an existing parking lot for 1400 automobiles to function as an ecologically based treatment system. 3D model generated in Form Z. Surface materials, trees and lighting elements are overlaid in Adobe Photoshop. By Peter Bednar.

17.8
The Red Fall Room, Garden of Trees for Two Rivers Park, Little Rock. Eye-level perspective focuses on lighting, spacing and textural effects applied to compose a landscape room. Basic perspective guidelines are established in AutoCAD. Landscape elements, lighting and surface textures are created in Adobe Photoshop. By John McWilliams.

17.9
South Shared Street Plaza for Porchscapes Housing. An axonometric drawing showcasing a neighborhood node in which the street is designed to function less like a dedicated corridor and more like a garden from building front to building front. 3D model generated in Google SketchUp and rendered using Lightscape. Line weights are exported from Google SketchUp and overlaid onto rendered image. Landscape elements and figures (people) are overlaid in Adobe Photoshop. By Jody Verser.

17.10 a–c
2030 scenario plan for Fayetteville Hilltown. Masterplan of hilltop site development (a), accompanied by perspective drawings showcasing scenarios for intensifying floodplains below as large catchments (b–c). 3D model generated in Autodesk Revit. Landscape elements are added in Photoshop. By Bart Kline.

17.11
2030 scenario plan for Fayetteville Transit City. Ground-level perspective drawing depicts transit-oriented development along a five-lane arterial that produces a dense, mixed-use, multimodal corridor. 3D model generated in Google SketchUp and rendered using V-Ray. Surface materials, landscape elements and people are overlaid in Adobe Photoshop. By Matthew Hoffman.

17.12
2030 scenario plan for Fayetteville Education City. Ground-level perspectives focus on the central role of corridor design in creating a high-quality pedestrian environment. 3D models – including landscape and people – generated in Google SketchUp and rendered using V-Ray. By Daniel Kuehn.

18 Envisioning Landscapes

Daniel Roehr with Matthew Beall

Drawing can't be taught, but it can be learned.

Laurie Olin[1]

To sketch is to draw from a position, to come to the page with a particular sensibility. Many experienced architects and instructors value the sketch as more than a visual record of ideas. For the adept, sketching is an unconstrained practice that not only documents ideas, but tests, explores, refines and communicates them. As a mode of visual thinking, sketching is a process that we use to work through problems, explore concrete and abstract subjects, record observations, organize data, contain and elaborate complexity, distinguish relationships, follow and verify intuitions, and spur creativity. It is a way of working that embraces the multiple – we can refine, vary, iterate as drawings demand – and that possesses no obligations of viewpoint, convention, technique or composition.

Despite its qualities, however, the habit of sketching is difficult to learn. The challenge is twofold: first, productive sketching requires a well-developed interrelationship between the hand, the senses and the mind; and second, sketching is difficult to teach.

The foremost goal in working with students learning to sketch is to impart a facility with the speed, versatility and openness of sketch-based visual thinking. At the University of British Columbia we encourage students to observe, play, take risks, and find pleasure in a process that, in the end, we hope becomes a habit that allows them to communicate with confidence, progress in design, and invest themselves in their representations and their products. To achieve this (admittedly ambitious) end, our strategy has been simple: challenge students from the very beginning to draw rich, complex subject matter – and to do it repeatedly. By beginning to sketch in dense urban environments or by observing masterworks of architecture and landscape, students are forced to filter and interpret what they observe and what they place on the page. As they work, struggle, re-work, and see their results, students almost always grow in confidence and ambition – they make more subtle observations, analyze more deeply, take more chances, and invest themselves in their work. While such sketchwork emphasizes hand-drawing, and the students tend to prosper when released from the specificity of digital tools, we set no limits on the media students employ. We encourage experimentation and mixed-media work, especially where students have a facility with digital tools that allows them to work with some speed and flexibility. The greatest successes in this strategy are often found in the work of students whose insecurities about technique or critique have been subsumed by their expanding vision and confidence in their ability to process those observations by gesture of the hand.

From presentation drawings on to precision work, students are reminded to look to their sketches for guidance. Those students who can transfer the better aspects of their sketchwork to other modes of drawing – whether it is clarity, fearlessness, conceptual strength, experimentation, or simply a compelling hand-rendering technique – tend in our experience to produce the most convincing and novel finished work. Some of the best representation works often tend to be the combination of hand-drawing and digital production tools using a flatbed scanner. The ability for students to bring their manual work into digital space affords them the opportunity to extend the potential of their hand-drawings. Once converted, students are able to duplicate, manipulate and layer their hand-drawings in order to use them as inputs for their digital tools or to augment and extend their digital representations. We have seen CAD drawings, 3D models, digital painting, photography and animation be productively combined with hand-drawn work, often with visually powerful results. In digital production (increasingly the norm in studio work), every object can always be manipulated – lines can be deleted or thickened at will, layers flipped on and off, time of day changed instantly. The students who treat a hand-drawing as one more object for manipulation in the digital work flow often surprise themselves and others with the way their manual outputs inform the development of their designs and the quality of their final outputs.

In many of today's landscape architecture studios, students are asked to work within complex urban environments. On these sites, the designer's task lies somewhere within a web of relationships between landscape architecture, ecology, architecture, urban planning, infrastructure development, cultural phenomena and political discourse. These sites demand multivariate analyses and often generate a large amount of graphic data. The challenge for students working on these projects is not only to filter and analyze complex inputs and constraints, but also to represent this complexity in a meaningful way in their work. Particularly successful drawings produced in this setting are those that judiciously layer traditional drawings and associated information, a process that often involves students devising new visual strategies of mixing non-spatial data into spatial representations. This type of work has the added benefit for students of clarifying the relationships not only within the project at hand, but also between different drawing types and techniques to goals of representation.

Note

1   Olin, L. "More than Wriggling Your Wrist (or Your Mouse): Thinking, Seeing and Drawing" in Treib, M. (ed.) *Drawing/Thinking, Confronting an Electronic Age*. London and New York: Routledge, 2008, p. 82.

18.1
Google SketchUp model drawing combined with Photoshop rendering, with highlighted area depicting sunset atmosphere for a privately owned villa in southern France. By Jia Cheng.

18.2 a–d
Clockwise from top left: (a) quick charcoal sketch over a SketchUp wireframe outline; (b) Photoshop rendering, summer scene with a painting used for the sky; (c) Photoshop rendering at night with white-light spots; (d) Photoshop rendering, winter scene. By James Johnson.

18.3 a–c
From top to bottom:
(a) charcoal drawing
on textured paper;
(b) Prismacolor
marker rendering
on plain paper; (c)
graphite sketch on
good quality paper.
By Sheena Soon.

18.4
Quick sketch using graphite and directional pencil stroke. By James Godwin.

18.5–18.9
A collection of sketch work produced by a group of architecture and landscape architecture students from the University of British Columbia while visiting northern and central Italy. Sketch work formed part of the students' observational, analytical hand-drawing in earnest for the first time. The sketches were made as the group visited a number of rich historical and contemporary sites.

18.5
Valsanzibio Giardino, Villa Barbarigo, near Padua, Italy. Digital composition; pencil, color pencil, digital annotation; this series of diagrammatic sketches was scanned and digitally arranged to present a well-composed analysis of scale and perspective within the famous Baroque garden. By David Guenter.

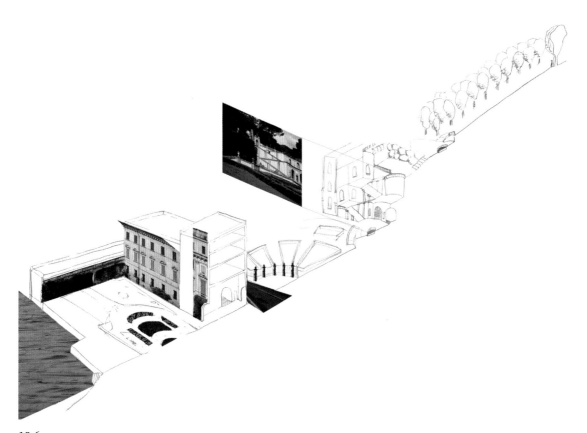

18.6
Villa Bettoni, Gargnano, Italy. Pen, digital collage; using a simple method of photo collage, this student has added considerable interest and meaning to a sectional axonometric sketch. The facility of this technique speaks to the potential for mixed-media sketching, where the exploratory, generative possibilities of sketching are not eclipsed by the specificity and technical demands of digital tools. By Hendrick Guliker.

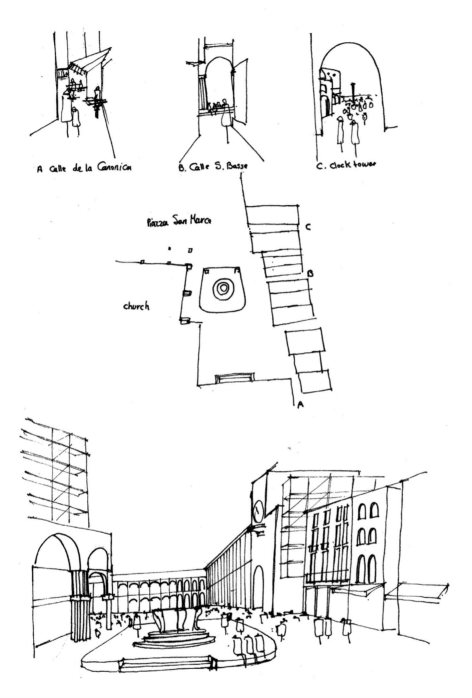

18.7
Piazza San Marco, Venice, Italy. Pen. Using a simply constructed perspective sketch, the student has constructed a concise analysis of an aspect of the urban transitions to the piazza. By Sara Kasaei.

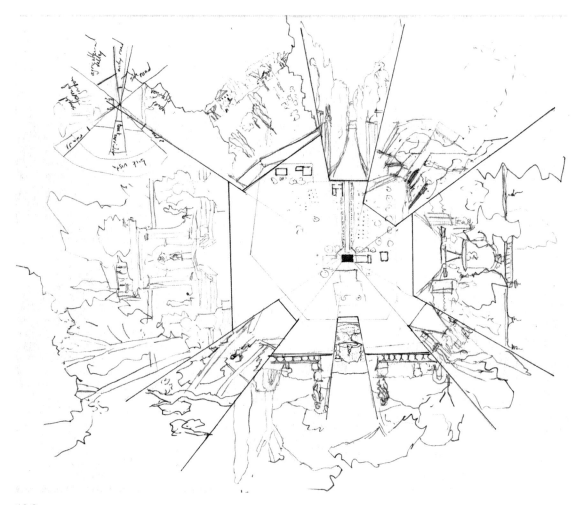

18.8
Villa La Pietra, Florence, Italy. Pencil. This sketch is a convincing investigation of the principal views from the Villa La Pietra. Composed of a number of perspective sketches, arranged in a radial manner and scaled according to their relation to the experience of the villa plan. By Matthew Beall.

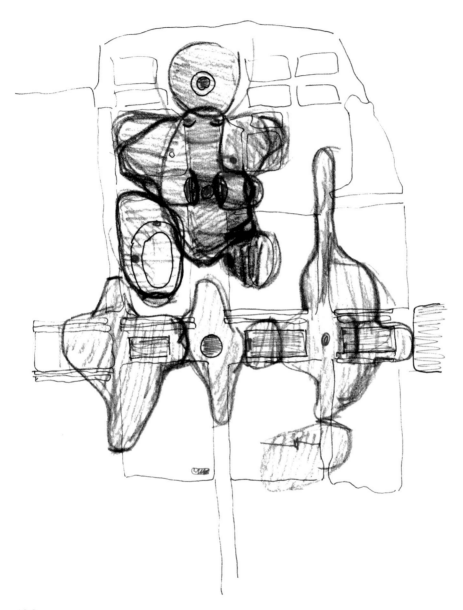

18.9
Valsanzibio Giardino, Villa Barbarigo, near Padua, Italy. Pen, colour pencil. This diagram
maps the sound of water within the Baroque garden. This sketch led to the insight that aural
experience played a role in the design of the garden, its materiality and the disposition of its
features. By Ariel Mieling.

19 The Art of Representing Landscapes

Chip Sullivan

> First strive in drawing to represent your intention to the eye by expressive forms, and the idea originally formed in your imagination.
>
> Leonardo da Vinci[1]

I have selected these projects (by students at the College of Environmental Design, University of California, Berkeley) because they exhibit unique and innovative approaches to the realm of landscape architectural representation. They are all provocative and push the boundaries of landscape architecture to an artistic level. This work covers a wide range of design problems, from traditional to contemporary gardens, abandoned railways, bioremediation and energy-conserving landscapes. Interestingly, a majority of my recent students have revealed a strong desire to express their work more artistically. Employing new methods of representation, such as handmade books, storyboards and three-dimensional constructions, their design projects have been rendered masterfully with a variety of media from pencil, pen-and-ink, watercolor and digital tools.

I have always believed that landscape architecture is an art form and should be accepted as such. I teach all of my classes through an artistic lens, with each student encouraged to develop his or her own sources of intuition, inspiration and imagination. Each project brief establishes a framework that allows exploration and pushes students to develop their individual creative processes. I try to facilitate a studio environment that functions as did a Renaissance *atelier* – a spontaneous community promoting the exchange of ideas, the sharing of graphic techniques, music, theory and philosophy. An important foundation of my teaching methodology is the incorporation of life drawing. I believe it is essential for designers to understand how a figure moves and animates the landscape. Unique to the format of my classes are studio visits, field trips to art exhibits and galleries, and end-of-term public exhibitions that give students a real sense of accomplishment.

Each project brief has specific media required for final presentation. The initial projects are rendered in black-and-white (pencil, then pen-and-ink): subsequent projects are rendered in color (colored pencil, followed by watercolor). Each medium is introduced with a hands-on demonstration and required practice exercises. There is an increasing level of difficulty to each exercise as the semester progresses. Students are required to keep a sketchbook in which they draw images from my lectures and document their thought process for each assignment. The goal is for them continually to record their ideas, inspirations and environments.

My studio pedagogy firmly establishes drawing as a tool for visualizing the design process. Sketch studies are used at all levels in the creative process. Each project begins with quick thumbnail studies of concepts that are then worked into storyboards, illustrating themes and sensations. Diagrams are drawn to scale and refined through the use of overlays. When a specific concept has emerged from the stacks of tracing paper, it is then studied and explored further through sections, elevations and perspectives. Physical evidence of the design process is a major element in the evaluation process. Final presentations must be composed as total visual ensembles of graphic communication.

That which fills my head and my heart must be expressed in drawing.

Vincent van Gogh[2]

Notes

1   Richter, I.A. (ed.) *The Notebooks of Leonardo da Vinci.* Oxford: Oxford University Press, 1980, p. 226.
2   Stone, I. (ed.) *Dear Theo: The Autobiography of Vincent van Gogh.* New York: Plume, 1995, p. 82.

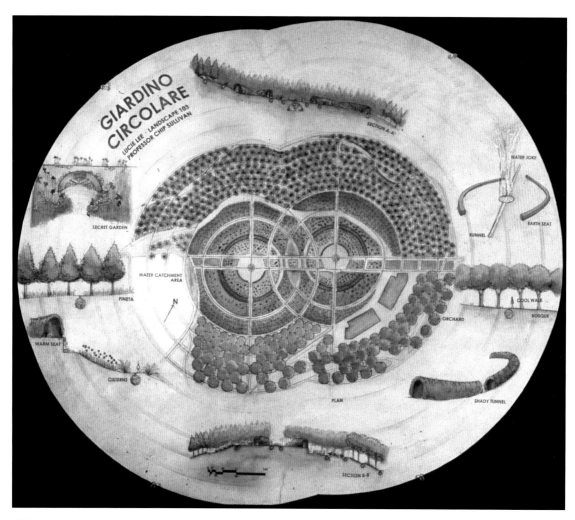

19.1

Giardino Circolare. This is a unique presentation for a sustainable landscape in the hills of Woodside, California. The page composition reflects the topography of the site plan. Additionally, the black background of the page helps to accentuate the unusual design. The opaque use of the watercolor in the plan view reinforces the patterns of the site plan and its circulation of water collection and distribution. The renderings along the circumference of the site plan are delightfully eye-catching. By Lucie Lee.

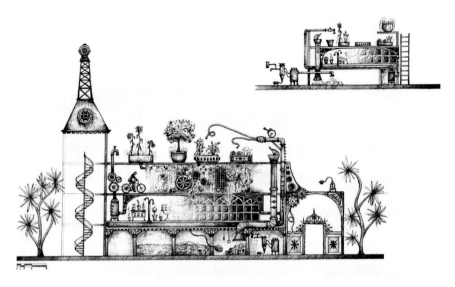

19.2

A Vertical Steampunk Garden. A vertical steam-powered garden, with a rooftop vegetable garden and composting system to produce energy to power the garden. The watercolor paper was first antiqued with a sepia-toned background. The drawing was created with elegant pen-and-ink cross-hatching. This is a very rich and expressive illustration with an amazing amount of detail that one can study for hours. The elevations have a realistic sense of depth, and portray a Victorian atmosphere that is a joyful place to explore. By Justine Holtzman.

19.3 a–d

Blake Garden Red Book. Using the precedent of Repton's *Red Books*, the students hand-made a large book (12 × 12'') to illustrate before-and-after views of their design proposals for a planting design studio. This project integrates the graphics and book-making techniques taught in an advanced landscape drawing class. This project specifically illustrates the potential of integrating craft, hand-drawing and watercolor with digital methods. With the use of paper engineering, cutouts and mover overlays, the students were able to depict before-and-after views. By Alex Harker Cecil Howell.

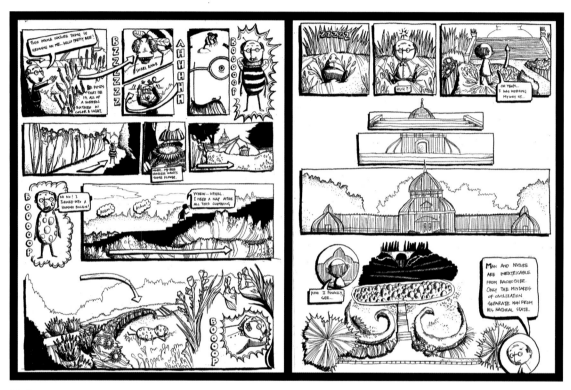

19.4

Story-boarding the Landscape. Black-and-white storyboards were assigned to explore the various ways in which one might move through a proposed design. This storyboard technique is used to help students visualize their design before drawing in plan, section and elevation. This is a very clear design scenario, rendered with strong black-and-white contrasts, combined with smooth visual flow and well-defined detail. It also captures movement through the design with a sophisticated use of establishment shots, close-ups, pans, fades, tracking shots and panorama. By Iris Chang.

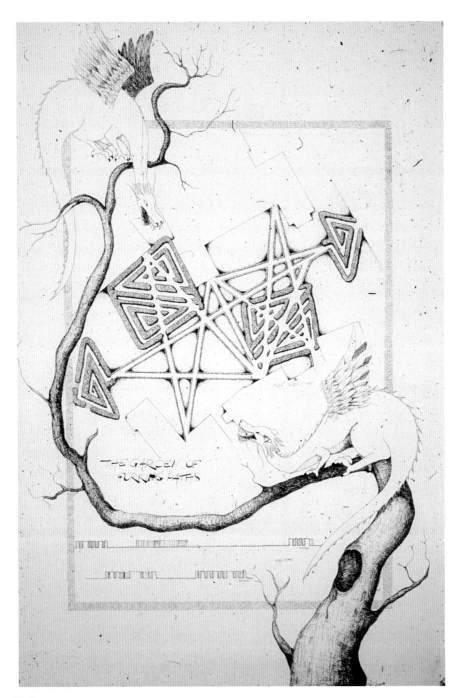

19.5

Garden of Forking Paths. For this project, the student was assigned to design a labyrinth based on the short story by Jorge Borges, "The Garden of Forking Paths". This is a masterful graphic design with a striking composition. The borders accent the texture of the maze, while the tree and dragons form a strong diagonal that captures the viewer's attention, drawing them into the composition. The maze is rendered to engage the eye to follow the circuit of the labyrinth as if you were walking within it. By Mari Carson.

20 The Significance of Texture

Anthony Mazzeo

Fundamental to the education of the landscape architect is the development of a critical understanding of the relationship between drawing and ground. The formal elements of drawing (line, tone, texture, etc.) applied to the drawing conventions most often used by the landscape architect (plan, section, perspective, etc.) play a significant role in how a designer's ideas are realized. How a designer develops, demonstrates and communicates design thought is most certainly linked to this application. Of course, potential discrepancies will always exist between the drawing medium and the landscape medium, but perhaps a way of narrowing that gap is to consider the drawing itself as a kind of surrogate terrain, a middle-ground mediating between process and product. Over the many years of helping aspiring landscape architecture students learn to draw, I have noticed that nowhere in the drawing process is that mediation more profound than in exploring the significance of texture, a shared term belonging to both worlds of drawing and landscape.

The late French philosopher Jacques Derrida believed the way a visually impaired person feels his/her way through space is an "allegory of drawing itself, of the draftsman's hands, as if someone had replaced the blind man's stick with the draftsman's pen" – seeing with one's hands, seeing prosthetically, feeling one's way through space not with eyes but with hands and sticks, with pencil and paper.[1]

In the Derridean sense, "to draw is to actually go blind to the press of perceptual presence and surrender the pen and paper to the world that is instituted in the dark as it were"[2] – the unseen that, for the landscape architect, is the yet-to-be-realized. This is especially relevant considering that landscape architectural drawing comes prior to construction.

Derrida's allegory of drawing is a useful teaching tool. First, it challenges the way designers typically place primacy on seeing over other modes of experience. Second, it points towards the relationship that exists between our senses of sight and touch.

According to Edward Casey, we physically experience the immediate character of a landscape through the "sensuous qualities of the surface it turns toward us."[3] The sensuous qualities are of many sorts, including primary and secondary qualities. Primary qualities include motion, shape and color. Secondary qualities, perhaps less familiar, include density, luminosity and, especially, texture.[4]

The significance of texture, relative to the making of landscape, is (in Edward Casey's phrase) its peculiar tangibility, both in the landscape and drawing medium:

> Texture embodies the peculiar tangibility, or feel, of wilderness ... What is at stake in the textuality of a wild place's sensuous surface is above all its inherent palpability, which is the most effective basis for coming to know the place's distinctive configuration, its physiognomy ... Palpitation and vision and kinesthesia often combine synesthetically, to be joined, perhaps, by audition and olfaction: we sense sounds as emanating from certain surfaces, and odors as clinging to them. Only by means of surface texture can the full sensuousness of a wildscape, its abundant changing-environing appearing, come into our ken.[5]

One of the ways this peculiar tangibility or feel comes through a drawing is through the use of frottage – the act of capturing what lies below the drawing surface, which, in the case of the landscape drawing, is the earth itself. Also, it is through frottage that the space separating the landscape and drawing medium is literally paper thin. Casey describes frottage as a "fabric of signification" in the following passage:

> This surface is a highly tactile sense of visual traces, none of which is indexical, much less symbolic. The effect is almost that of a self-absorbed icon. I say "almost." For in fact there is an allusion to something else literally underneath the drawing, namely, the rugged mass of what is placed under the work, which the drawing traces out compulsively. This is rock or sand or some other substance – something that belongs to the natural world.[6]

Texture is a quality of both the material world of landscape and the virtual world of drawing. Therefore the significance of texture relative to drawing landscape is the way it prompts the memory and triggers the imagination of both author and reader alike.

The following were produced by students at the College of Architecture and Planning, University of Colorado, Denver.

Notes

1   Caputo, J. *The Prayers and Tears of Jacques Derrida: Religion Without Religion.* Bloomington, IN: Indiana University Press, 1997, p. 315.
2   Caputo, 1997, *op. cit.*, p. 319. The entire passage continues: "He must let the thing itself slip away, break with tyranny of what is present, with the visible, perceptual presence which would otherwise paralyze his pen. Moving with lightning speed, his pen is carried on the wings of memory, which serves as a shutter which instantly, in the instant includes and excludes, sorts among a riot of too much detail which it must see no more, including and enlarging this, excluding and diminishing that. To draw is to go blind to the press of perceptual presence and surrender the pen and paper to the world that is instituted in the dark as it were".
3   Casey, E.S. "The arc of desolation and the array of description," in *Getting Back Into Place:*

Toward a Renewed Understanding of the Place-World. Bloomington, IN: Indiana University Press, 1993, p. 209.

4 Casey, 1993, *op. cit.*
5 Casey, 1993, *op. cit.*, p. 210.
6 Casey, E.S. "Plotting and charting the path: voyaging to the ends of the Earth with Michelle Stuart," in *Earth-Mapping: Artists Reshaping Landscape*. Minneapolis, MN: University of Minnesota Press, 2005, p. 59.

manipulation: regrading, reseeding to produce desired consequences and experiences

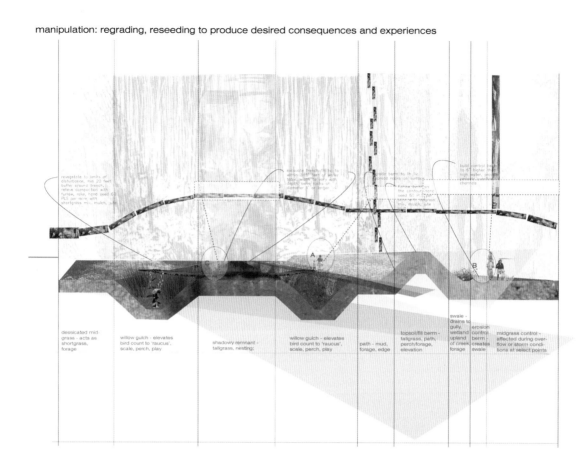

Using the cut as the initiator of all further process on site, several new conditions are possible. The cut itself alters the hydrology of the western portion of the site from that of sheeting to a more direct, conventional drainage pattern. This effectively desicates the grassland, altering its performance from that of midgrass to that of shortgrass prairie. By concentrating water, the cut also helps to perpetuate the willow. The willow provides habitat for birds, a spot for play and discovery for children, and a place of comfort or interest for humans due to its color and the created enclosure. The fill, a byproduct of the cut, creates new habitat as well by dividing the northern section of the field from the southern. This maintains the hydrology of the nothern portion, allowing the grasses there to remain tall — perfect for nesting. The berm itself is revegetated with sandhills prairie grassland species to provide a marker of change on the landscape. The whole operation creates a large zone of impact which allows for new seedings and can potentially spur succession by disturbing the the dominance of the highly alleopathic wheat. This operation also introduces numerous edges along which to walk and explore allowing for new zones of privacy and exposure, discovery and contemplation. The point of all this is to understand that in any project there is a chance to make minor decisions with potentially major impacts. Where to cut, where to fill, what to reseed with, how high, how wide, etc. can all add up to a new and intersting landscape, a byproduct of development.

20.1

Presentation drawing – mixed media, collage, section-perspective images. By Lindsay Cutler.

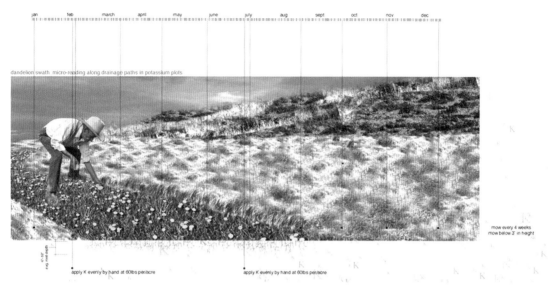

20.2

Exploring notions of creating pattern (planting pattern) by altering nutrient applications to various plots, collage perspective. Black-and-white with color element aspects and indexing notes. By Kelly Smith.

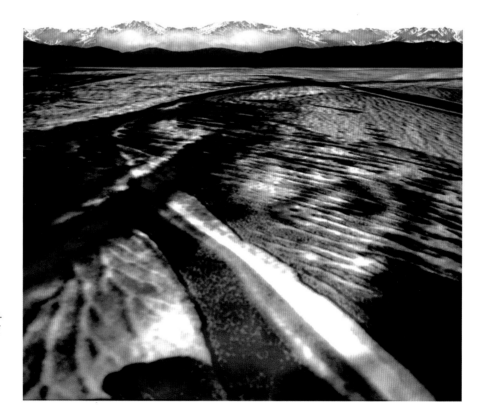

20.3

Wetland perspective. Photograph of relief model collaged into site image, Photoshop. By Erin Devine.

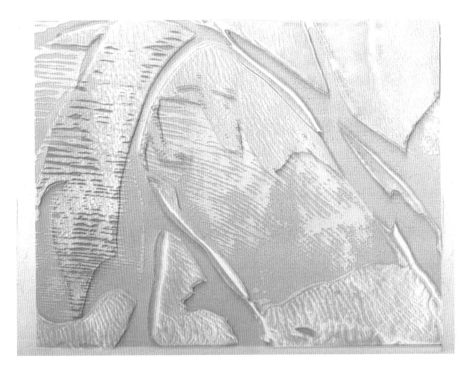

20.4
Relief model representing garden plots. Using wood, Plexiglas, museum board crafted through computer numerical control (CNC) process. By Erin Devine.

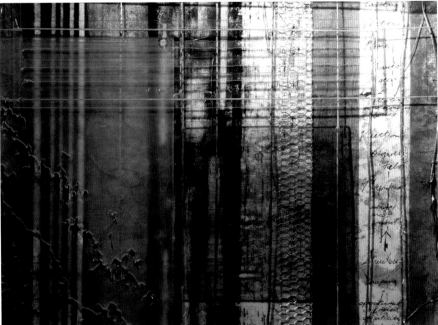

20.5
Experimental drawing/collage attempting to simulate land-forming processes through a variety of drawing techniques, including charcoal rubbings (frottage), acrylic paint, Plexiglas and wire. Here the student attempts to create a range of graphic marks, analogues to various landscape processes such as erosion and deposition, as a means to evoke specific characteristics of the site. By Doug Kay.

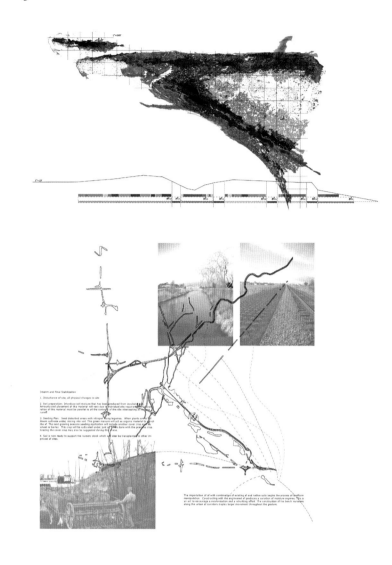

20.6 a–d
A final presentation panel, combination of drawings including plan, linking to perspectives, photographic drawings and section-elevations. By Joe Kuk.

21 Visual Facilitation

Sean Kelly

I believe to facilitate drawing is to facilitate communication. If students are offered the governing concepts, processes and information, and then supervised as they develop these processes and experiment with making them their own, they will readily gain confidence as they learn and practise hand-drawing, computer-aided drawing, rendering and communicating skills. While I believe technology has in many ways both aided and hindered students' understanding and learning of the communication process, the contribution made by students in my courses at the University of Guelph, School of Environmental Design and Rural Development must be acknowledged for their valuable and tolerant assistance over the years. Their tenacity, suggestions, advice and criticism, both technical and personal, and, particularly, their commitment to becoming more proficient with technology has resulted in some truly outstanding products.

While there are too many images to include in this book, the landscape architectural student work included, at both undergraduate and graduate levels, offers a glimpse into several recent successes capitalizing on the combination of various styles, media and techniques. In general, most of these images use technology to their advantage to first set up then render a project, and then to select particular views and/or compose layouts – all requiring the student to think about what it is necessary to show. The majority of the Guelph images are situated in urban landscapes, hence the media selected and utilized are versatile in effectively demonstrating site context. In addition, an ability to bring together resourcefulness, proficiency in varying software programs (including several open-source or freeware options), attention to detail, and an understanding of the time available for producing these resulted in truly effective communication drawings. It is notable that each of the students involved in the work presented here also had a good ability in "hand graphics", and this has been exercised in the storyboarding of these works.

In our studios, drawing and communicating graphics are seen as two separate activities. Students are guided from the beginning of their time at Guelph to evolve their ideas graphically before their drawing skills (and computer skills) reach a quality level. Many of the faculty have used exercises that are designed for instant initial success in "thinking" about design and generating ideas. Thus the process of seeing and practising, necessary to progress through the more challenging aspects of graphic communication, is set in motion early in the program. Guiding towards restraint students often concerned only with "making drawings look good" (learning software, techniques) in lieu of generating defendable ideas is often a difficult aspect of the process, yet a necessary activity in the studio courses.

Key to many of these images is the message of the illustration, or what a student is trying to communicate: this is what determines all aspects of a graphic, its viewpoint, size, priority or importance, quality, and, most importantly, the time it will take to produce. Once the student has established the message of each drawing, the next objective is deciding how a series of drawings might work together to form a presentation. With these preliminary aspects of the communication process in place, a student can then focus on preparing the final presentation graphics, hence selecting the most appropriate media to convey the message. The most important concept related to technique, or style, of the graphic is that these drawings evolved through an additive process; the graphic is developed by adding a series of successive layers of media and quality until the appropriate priority level is reached.

Personally, I have been a student of graphics, formally, since 1984. I believe I was set on the journey to successful teaching by many: Lari Wester and his Design Communication for Landscape Architects, Mike Lin, Michael Doyle, Ted Walker, Grant Reid and Jim Leggitt, to name a few favorites. Much of my commitment to facilitating the learning of graphic media and style has been acquired from the fear and frustration that I experienced as a new student of landscape architecture; I owe many – most of these being the students themselves.

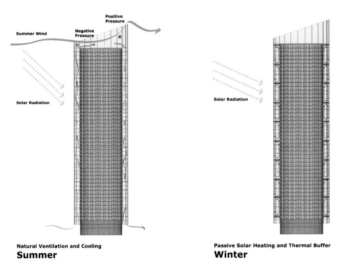

Natural Ventilation and Cooling
Summer

Passive Solar Heating and Thermal Buffer
Winter

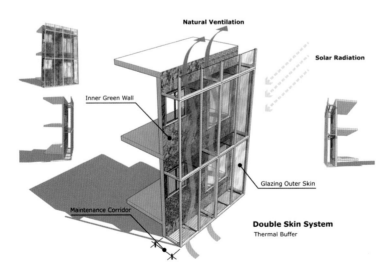

21.1–21.6
MLA thesis project for Toronto urban waterfront, redevelopment strategies for East Bayfront. All illustrations generated with AutoCAD base and SketchUp 3D (buildings); foreground park site and lake rendered with Vue 6 Landscape Visualization by e-on. This software enabled 3D trees and plants to appear realistic and detailed. Advanced rendering tools permit photorealistic water with accurate transparency and reflectivity, as well as surface and depth colors with adjustable murkiness. They also enable stunning atmosphere with volumetric cloud layers and realistic haze. By Yang Huang.

Landform

Drops of water on the land

Forest and Wetland

Forest establishment process

Landform
"Water wave"

Pioneer species mature
Long-living species sprout

Seed
Pioneer species @ "wave" crest
Long-living species @ "wave" trough

Long-living species mature
Core establish

Pioneer species sprout

Core expand

Landform
Drop of water

Coastal Wetland
Seed

Rocky Edge

Landform
Cutting

Coastal Wetland
Sprout

Rocky Edge
Multiply

Landform
Water

Coastal Wetland
Adapt

Coastal Wetland
Multiply

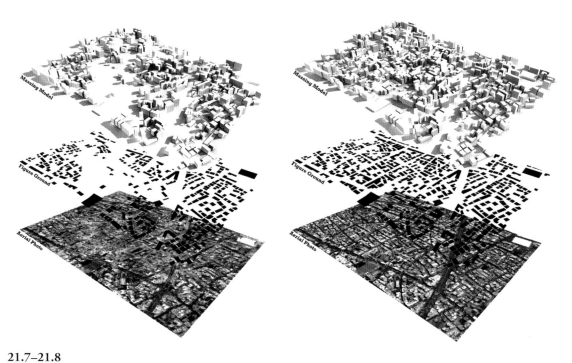

21.7–21.8
Urban design, high-density development for Haret District, Beirut. "Exploded view" comprised of aerial photography,
figure ground in AutoCAD, and SketchUp 3D model to render the building massing (21.7). Plan view graphic generated
in SketchUp 3D and rendered as a digital watercolor in Photoshop; character sketches generated in SketchUp 3D and
rendered as a digital watercolor in Photoshop, providing a "hand-crafted" look (21.8). By Brian Caccio.

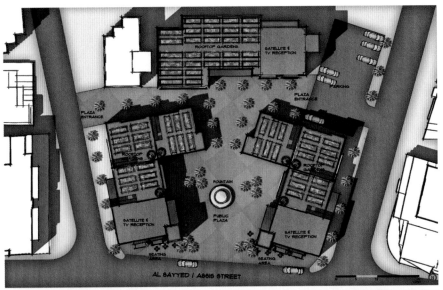

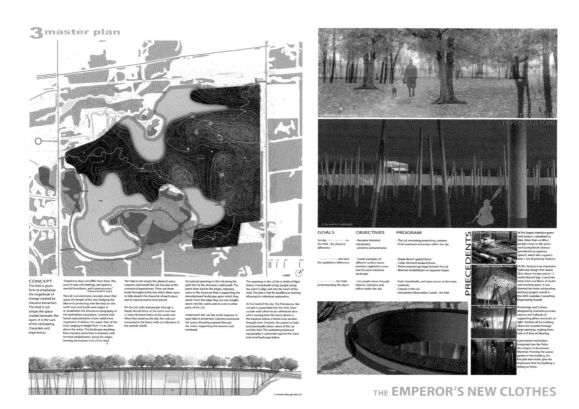

21.9–21.10

Master plan aggregate site/rehabilitation scheme. "The Emperor's New Clothes" gives form to the void resulting from aggregate-extraction activities. The void is not simply the space created between the layers; it is the sum of the contrasting characters and experiences. Plan view graphic prepared with AutoCAD and rendered with Photoshop. Corresponding section and character sketches prepared with Google SketchUp. By Jan Jurgensen, Audric Montuno and Eryn Buzza.

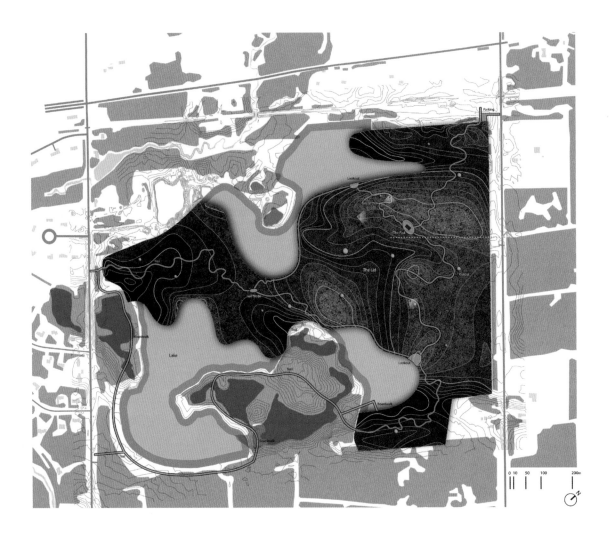

21.11–21.12
Urban Plaza
Core, Toronto.
Bird's-eye view and
perspective sketch
generated from an
AutoCAD base,
which was imported
into SketchUp
3D for massing
and exported to
Kerkythea, an
open-source/freeware
rendering program.
Background
buildings rendered
from reference
photograph. By
Stephen Heller.

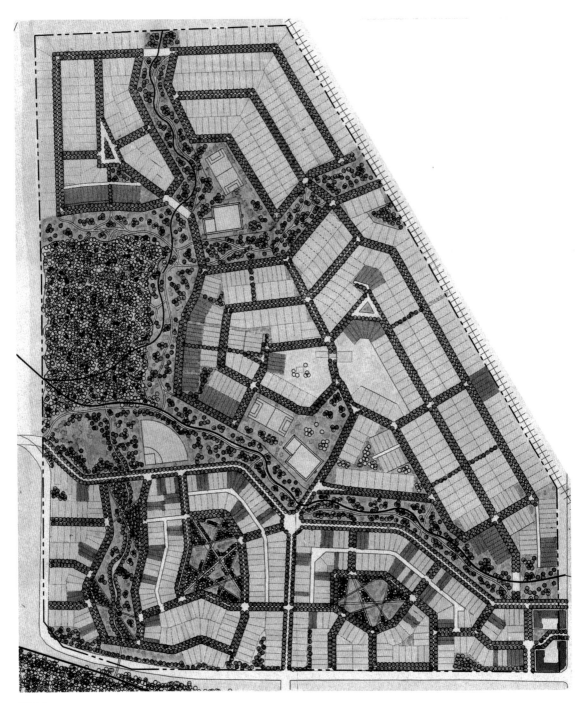

21.13
Community design, master plan for a rural/agricultural setting. Plan view graphic developed with a base plan generated in AutoCAD, plotted onto vellum and hand-rendered with Chartpak markers. By Matt Williams, Yang Huang and Daniel Irving.

21.14 a–b
UG image:
industrial/warehouse
district. "The City
of Kitchener's
Green Light
District: An Urban
Metamorphosis"
(2011) explores the
ideas of combining
functionality, art
and nature in a
post-industrial
area's redesign that
benefits humans and
the environment.
Colored pencil over
ink pen. Using trace
paper, a perspective
was drawn from an
existing site photo.
The perspective was
then photocopied
onto bond paper
and colored pencil
was added. The
completed colored
drawing was scanned
and assembled
into panels with
Illustrator software,
where additional
rendering and
touch-ups were
done. By Jaclyn
Marsh.

22 On Landscape Architecture, Design and Drawing from the Broken Middle

Marcella Eaton and Richard Perron

Is landscape a verb? Architecture is understood as a verb [adverb], not a noun, in this context. Architecture is not what we make, but what we do. This does not diminish the product or places created by the act of architecture, but it does shift attention toward the educational pedagogy as a way of doing. Is this an all-encompassing theory? Perhaps, however, this thinking is directed toward the actors in the network of teachers, students and things – the network of places, memories and desires.

Students in our studios (in the Department of Landscape Architecture at the University of Manitoba) are encouraged to think of visual representation as an act of transitive thinking in the process of design. We are interested in having the work move beyond expectations of normative solutions, and helping students to move beyond even their own expectations. Students dwell in the process of their thoughts made manifest in drawing.

Part of teaching landscape architecture is more about finding ways of coping with the complexities of the everyday, deliberately engaging in actions of rematerializing human/non-human worlds, worlds of intersecting desires, worlds that are as much about beauty and pleasure as they are about performance and function. In our work, we are seeking hybrid/connective/authentic design solutions that deal with shifting spatial conditions and the events that define our landscapes. Landscapes are, by their very nature, restless. Can the act of drawing subvert the fixity of representation? Is there a way to draw and not fix the idea of world, space and place? Is this what we do when we try to create atmosphere, mood and passion in a design and subsequent drawing, or are we simply trying to fixate the intangible? We ask students to question what this means in relation to their work. We try to disrupt their belief that the skill of drawing, including both analogue and digital, is simply a communication technique; rather, it can provide an opportunity as a process of discovery, often drawing as a restless search for revealing the opportunities of site. We argue that drawing is not simply depiction of an object, but an act of searching for an expression of a transitive condition. Transitive drawing is an investigation for that which is intangible and in flux, revealing a condition of landscape change and landscape process.

To this end, landscape designers could, to use Bruno Latour's term, serve as reliable witness to human–non-human exchanges, speaking for [representing] non-human and human concerns, and designing not only landscapes, but also ways to test the faithfulness of landscape representations.[1]

Within the landscape, text and context are assimilated into an amalgam of change and choice. Places circulate with the desires, deformations and reformulations of the everyday. Places are not simply what we make, but also what we make of them, circulating in the texts and memories of intersecting narratives. Landscape architecture, then, is a form of recording, a recording of intersecting tendencies and desires, a recording of the affects of entities and of the affordances of place. Landscape architecture is not about the mummified recording of the moment of observation; instead, it might be thought of as a means of capturing latent identity in process, assemblages of ways of seeing latent potential. Landscape architecture is about living in spatial/social flux. Landscape is never fixed or stable, but always a continuing result of the processes of dialogic reclamation. We see landscape architecture as more than conceiving new spatial possibilities, but also as a form of ecocritique about the potential of place.

> Ecocritique could establish collective forms of identity that included other species and their world, real and possible. It would subvert fixating images of "world" that inhibit humans from grasping their place in an already historical nature. Subverting fixation is the radical goal of the Romantic wish to explore the shadow lands ... Subversion of identity fixations is what Alain Badiou calls a truth process, a rigorous and relentless distinction of the subject from its identifications ... The environment was born at exactly the moment when it became a problem ... Humans may yet return the idea of the "thing" to its older sense of meeting place. In a society that fully acknowledged that we were always already involved in our world, there would be no need to point it out.[2]

We ask students to not leave the past behind, but to investigate a break in the sense of the past, a break with meaning determined by, in this example, dominant industrial categories. This is a mediation often found by weaving the frames of past categorical imperatives into new categorical assemblages – factory as a place of play, industrial wasteland as garden site, a blending of the forces of industry with the forces of nature. This is a way of thinking and working from the broken middle.

> [T]o be in the middle, without "absolute beginning" is also a way of shaking free from circularity, releasing "what thinks" from the closed circle ... Isn't the self-consciousness of the middle, in the stream, the viewing of experience in terms of moments untethered from the absolute beginning, a way of restating the anxiety of the enclosing circle and absence of enclosure rather than of reaffirming the

circle? Perhaps aesthetic experience hovers between self-enclosed autonomy and the absence of frame?[3]

We also consider a poetic device, scansion. This can be translated into spatial terms when we think about where the emphasis lies, such as the choice of vistas, framing devices, enchantment and delight, even the sublime. Movement through a space can be seen as a playing through on accents, tone and texture, creating surprise, creating openings – the texture of a space. The other way of considering scansion is the mapping of design process, the mapping of the act of designing, of taking note of what you are doing while you do it. The question that must be asked is, how to work within the broken middle without taking away from the creative act? When is being critical distracting us from being creative? When does being overly critical hold us back? The answer might be about the affect, reason and confluence in which we constantly find ourselves. Returning to the example, the post-industrial may be seen as a way of framing this confluence, of opening possibilities not simply within the "designed product" but in the way we think about design. We wondered if this might help students to become more interested in landscape, in place, in life. How do we scan what we are doing when we do it?

> Sometimes the concept of scanning is also used to judge a poem: it may be said that a poem "scans well" if it controls the meeting between words, rhythm and meaning elegantly or convincingly; equally a poem does "not scan" if the words become stuck against the rhythm of the line, if their syllables clunk rather than ripple with the rhythm, or if the pause between words sit awkwardly with the pauses between beats. This is seen in "doggerel" poetry.[4]

How do we scan place? How do we scan place poetically? Many successful landscape architects clearly scan places, and scan conversations about places, to understand environments. Alexandre Chemetoff's text *Visits*[5] is an explicit example of this. We ask students, what strikes you? What has emotive power? What has affect?

In our work, we have been influenced by the theories on operational eidetics and the agency of mapping articulated by James Corner, but we believe these ideas warrant critical consideration. Eidetics can have a great power, but they can also get in the way when we become obsessed with the beauty of the image over the substance of the idea. Expressions, no matter how dynamic they become, never capture the thick richness of place. An articulation is a way of dealing with the complexity of change, translating entities, relationships and processes into forms and substance, codes and milieus. Representations themselves rarely provide insight into the nature of the process of becoming. In schools of design, drawings act as a way to reveal understanding, and for students to be understood. Drawings leave and cause marks; they leave and cause effects. Specific and unspecific ambiguity as a means of breaking with the fixity of an object, of seeing landscape as an object, is a way of breaking from the predictable. A transition from the "void" of the blank sheet through to expression of mood, feeling and space is created. We are less interested in drawings that try to fix space and object. We encourage drawings that release expressions of place. Drawings/maps/models are restless devices, transient modes of engaging spatio-temporal conditions. Drawings implicate the designer in ways of thinking, of moving through, and of tracing experiences and events.

Corner seems to prefer the notion of imaging to representation, and although the terms may seem synonymous, their differences may be best understood in terms of what they do, how they perform, their agency and design potential.[6] Images are thus the stuff of interaction, and design may be thought of as taking pause, reacting and deciding to influence the next collision of images, be that about the images on the landscape, or the images in the landscape itself. For Corner, it is not only the material of the built world that has agency, but also the design process of imaging. Imaging should not simply represent; it should evoke, actively causing us to think in certain ways. There is a direct correlation between the ways that we image things and our understanding. Imaging embeds us in a process of design uncovering, discovering and understanding. Imaging involves a wide range of techniques, including mapping, cataloguing, phasing, layering, etc., but more importantly we should be thinking about the agencies of techniques. What they do – images deployed to query, explore, reorganize perceptions and synthesize different insights, and how they might be used in conjunction with other design and planning activities – diagramming, organizing, assembling, merging, displacing, etc. This kind of work is often an amalgam of analytical thinking and process-oriented imaging. The way we image our landscapes and the ways we imagine how they can become are intertwined. We are interested in thinking about landscape in familiar terms, including soil, geomorphology, ecosystems, land use, land cover, habitation, circulation, topography, aspect, exposure, etc., and then drawing what might happen when these networks are in different states of movement. The work builds from descriptive and predictive modeling exercises using spatial information systems technologies. The acts of roaming, connecting, interrelating, assembling and moving are not simply limited to human activities, but involve the multiple webs of plant and animal communities as well as other physical assemblages. Connected landscapes are about bringing order to coherent fields – social, cultural, natural. This can be a multi-layered process, including the distillation and recombination of varying systems of movement and flows. This goes beyond the movement of people, money and goods, to reading and writing the landscape as the agent for the flow of a wide range of species and materials. Land, air, water are all potential media for landscape flow. One of the challenges of the designer is to interpret and assist in the emergence of coherent fields, to find ways to assimilate the multiple and sometimes conflicting paths and intersections between the flows of people, material and other species.

These surface strategies may be understood in terms of what Anuradha Mathur and Dilip da Cunha[7] refer to as designing with a shifting landscape. This includes designing for shifting programs and meandering spatial conditions, including changing flows and the continual displacement of landscape living and non-living materials. Surface strategies are designed to uncover and/or illustrate the shifting dynamic surface conditions.

The matter on which landscape architecture is made is, first and foremost, the drawing. Drawings have agency in their product as well as in the act of the becoming. As we learn to draw, we develop our own personal sets of functional and symbolic constraints. The movement of understanding and action in becoming a designer is energy that is equivalent to the product of drawing, working together.

Landscapes are conceived as dynamic and often unpredictable, and design is less about the elaboration of specifics than it is about the liberation of potential, of creating situations where new activities, uses and interactions may emerge. We continue to ask ourselves, and our students, can drawing be a way of preceding signification? Or does every drawing begin as a means to an end? Can drawing be a process of finding rather than a process of representing? Is the freedom and interpretation limited to the artifact, the physical drawing itself, the result of design thinking, or can freedom and interpretation be implicit in the energy of drawing? Does the motive force of architecture imply signification, or can the signifier be allowed to float in the act of drawing?

We often have the tendency to think of nature/ecology as some kind of 'other', that it is something outside the human realm. Instead, in our studios, we try to resist the tendency to objectify nature/ecology. Instead, nature/ecology is thought of as systems and networks, as interrelated processes understood through the uncovering of co-dependencies and interactions. Landscapes are restless – the restless workings of ecologies, the restless occupation of the land, the restless agitations of everyday life. Design, drawing, students, educators are all in a constant state of motion, in a continual state of becoming.

The environment is that which cannot be indicated directly. We could name it apophatically. It is not-in-the-foreground. It is the background caught up in a relationship with the foreground. As soon as we concentrate on it, it turns into the foreground ... The environment *is* the "what-is-it", the objectified version of our question. As soon as it becomes an exclamation it has disappeared."[8]

Notes

1   Latour, B. *Politics of Nature: How to Bring the Sciences into Democracy*. Cambridge, MA: Harvard University Press, 2004.

2   Morton, T. *Ecology Without Nature: Rethinking Environmental Aesthetics*. Cambridge, MA: Harvard University Press, 2007, p. 141.

3   Armstrong, I. *The Radical Aesthetic*. Oxford: Blackwell, 2000, p. 67.

4   Williams, R. *The Poetry Toolkit: The Essential Guide to Studying Poetry*. London: Continuum, 2009, p. 133.

5   Chemetoff, A. *Visits: Town and Territory – Architecture in Dialogue*. Basel: Birkhäuser Verlag AG, 2009.

6   Corner, J. "Operational eidetics forging new landscapes," *Harvard Design Magazine*, 6, Fall 1998; Corner, J. "The agency of mapping: speculation, critique, and invention," in *Mappings*, edited by Denis Cosgrove. London: Reaktion Books, 1999.

7   Mathur, A. and da Cunha, D. *Mississippi Floods: Designing A Shifting Landscape*. New Haven, CT: Yale University Press, 2001; Mathur, A. and da Cunha, D. at *Ecological Urbanism* conference, Harvard University Graduate School of Design, 3–5 April 2009.

8   Morton, 2007, *op. cit.*, p. 175.

9   McGrath, B. and Gardner, J. *Cinemetrics: Architectural Drawing Today*. New York: Wiley, 2007.

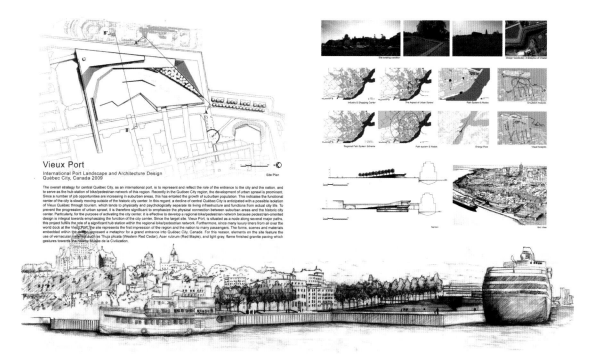

22.1

Panel, plan long section-perspective, diagrams, photos, sections, 3D aerial view drawing (aerial perspective) well composed on large panel board with descriptive text for Yoshi Vieux Port project. By Yoshi Yabe.

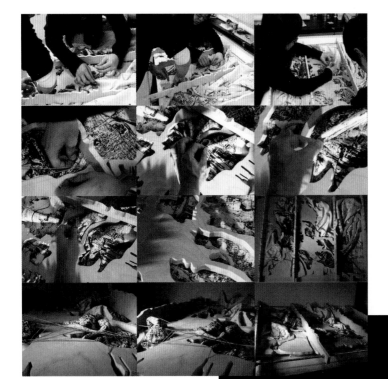

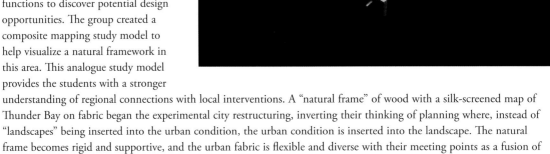

22.2

Composite study models and final model (analogue) for Thunder Bay, Ontario project. For this regional-scale project, students developed study models for Thunder Bay. The group felt there is a need to restructure the decaying urban fabric to sustain a thriving cultural and natural atmosphere. This model explicitly illustrates, and encourages stronger collaboration between, the "natural frame" with the necessary urban functions to discover potential design opportunities. The group created a composite mapping study model to help visualize a natural framework in this area. This analogue study model provides the students with a stronger understanding of regional connections with local interventions. A "natural frame" of wood with a silk-screened map of Thunder Bay on fabric began the experimental city restructuring, inverting their thinking of planning where, instead of "landscapes" being inserted into the urban condition, the urban condition is inserted into the landscape. The natural frame becomes rigid and supportive, and the urban fabric is flexible and diverse with their meeting points as a fusion of culture and nature. By Justin Neufeld, Tracy Liao and Yoshi Yabe.

22.3

Large perspective drawing for Ottawa, Ontario Project. For this drawing, the student uses a combination of photography, 3D digital modeling, graphite, and Photoshop for the rendering, used for its air-brushing capabilities. The student experiments with the combination of different media to bring a certain depth and movement into the rendering to reflect the nature of the design. The student tests the idea of how the "soft" natural progression of the sketch and the "anxious" precision of the computer can work in unison. By Justin Neufeld.

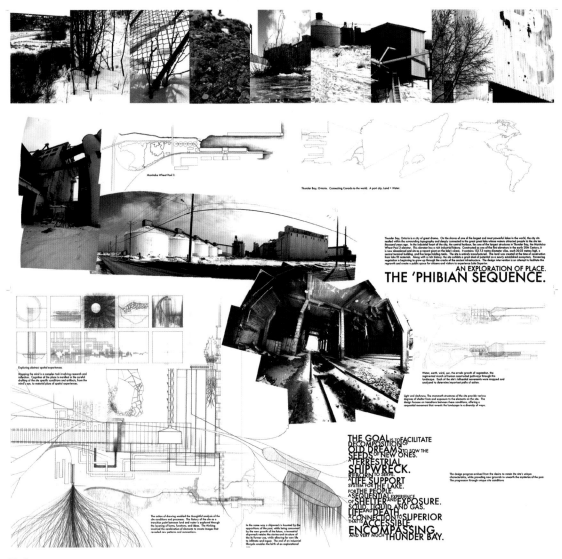

22.4

Environmental design project – sequence drawing for Thunder Bay area. Beautifully composed sequence drawings; the students use 2H, 4H and 6H lead on vellum on all these drawings for the Thunder Bay studio. The student also adds, "when drawing I am typically thinking about creating a visual hierarchy with the lines that are drawn. Lead in various degrees of hardness is useful in achieving dominant, subdominant, and subordinate elements within a composition. Rendering elements of the drawing can also be completed with the use of the shavings from the lead, creating areas of uniform cover. Vellum is a very flexible substrate to work upon. It has enough *tooth* to hold onto the lead, yet not so much that it is difficult to keep lines crisp and sharp. Its translucent quality makes it very useful for tracing or layering drawings. The flexibility of the material means that it is seldom limiting, and can be utilized for most projects. For this particular set of drawings, a layering of information became very important in order to showcase the ways in which the site conditions would shift over time. The use of lead and vellum was helpful in allowing the drawings to evolve over time, folding drawings over themselves and tracing earlier elements to create an intertwined fabric of images. As some of this imagery was more important than others, it was advantageous to be able to 'ghost in' particular sections by using a very hard lead. More than the ability to choose different thicknesses of ink liners, lead of different hardness creates a whole new feel for drawing and requires a very personal, mechanical, and methodical shift in the way one draws." By Shawn Stankewich.

22.5
Section of urban coastal area depicting high tide. By Meaghan Hunter.

22.6 a–b
Perspective, collage perspective for
New Orleans project. Beautiful
black-and-white tones, second
perspective adding subtle colour
– collage to depict further design
interventions. By Kristen Struthers.

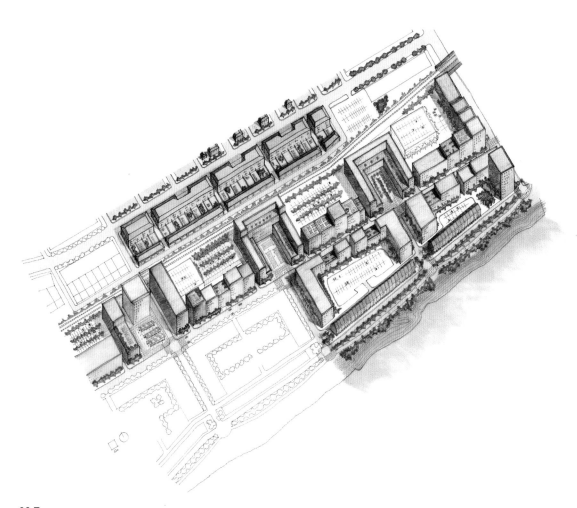

22.7

Large axonometric drawing. For this studio, students examine issues of infrastructure in the urban context. Students work together on the neighborhood scale and then independently to resolve issues within that context. The student has drafted the axonometric by hand with ink on vellum and has rendered it using pencils. Some urban block are left in plan, black-and-white. Provides good balance between fully colored rendered 3D-projected blocks. By Judith Cheung, Kaleigh Lysenko, Sarry Klein and Leah Rampton.

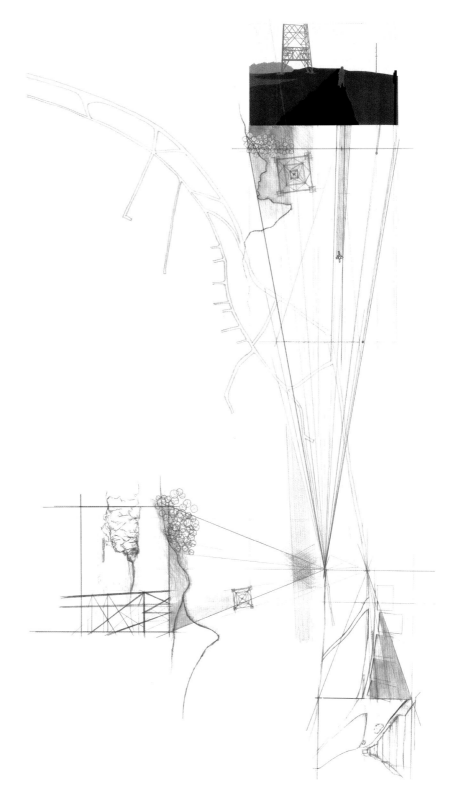

22.8

Expressional drawing for New Orleans project. The student has mapped and drawn personal experiences from a single point along the top of the levee along the Mississippi and framed several views. Drawing inspirations from McGrath and Gardner,[9] the setting quickly shifts by redirecting the view from the road running parallel to the river and levee, to the path at the top of the levee, and then to the river and batture. Using hand-drawing, drafting and Photoshop, the student believes that these media and techniques communicate much more about the complexity of the site. By Meaghan Pauls.

22.9 a–b

For "Theatre for the Apocalypse", Thunder Bay project. For this final design studio in the Environmental Design degree, students are asked to design their own brief, and are encouraged to communicate in a manner that they feel best represents the spirit of the work. For this drawing, the student certainly succeeded in this, using an abandoned grain elevator to create a theatre to witness the end of the world. This work was all completed by hand. The student offers, "for all the main ink drawings I used Arches 90 lb watercolor paper that I printed my original pen and pencil draftings on, then used India ink for washes and splotches. Any of the process work was usually done on trace with India ink, with oil pastels, and I think I used some Conté on a couple." Here the student has used a variety of techniques, including drafted, drawn and painted ink, and graphite, and much experimentation. By Aiden Stothers.

23 Visual Representation in Landscape Architecture

Karen M'Closkey

Landscape architects were pioneers in the digital revolution through the development of geographic information systems, a successor to the hand-drawn overlays of Eliot, Manning and McHarg. More recent advances in digital media have not yet been as well considered in landscape architecture in terms of their ability to transform working methods and what those methods might engender. Rather than see digital tools as replacements for their hand-drawn counterparts, new media should be considered for what they enable (and do not) in terms of landscape ideation. What distinguishes the latest technologies from previous innovations is their total integration into all phases of design and construction. It is precisely this multiplicity of roles that has allowed technology to profoundly transform contemporary practice by altering modes and standards of making.

Imaging and imagining

Tools for seeing (such as GPS, satellite imagery, Google, etc.) and expressing (such as surface modeling, parametrics, and numeric machines) have greatly expanded the techniques we use for design today. The former have enhanced our ability to obtain information, and the latter have provided a myriad of new ways to explore and express design. As such, there are no generally appropriate methods for landscape drawing; it all depends on the intent of the image, since image construction and conceptual content are inseparable. While this may seem self-evident, there are some grumblings about how digital technology has distanced us from seeing; however, digital technology and design do not alleviate the need to use and construct images with intent, nor do they displace manual drawing.

Digital technology will change how we see and construct images, and therefore how we see and construct landscapes. The question is: what opportunities might this afford? I think it offers great potential for new conceptions about the relationship between form and process, which is inherent in all landscapes. We understand the environment differently today than we did thirty years ago; we accept more complexity, and perhaps less control. Digital tools allow us to envision this complexity in new ways.

Visualizing versus viewing

There is a tendency today toward an over-reliance on photorealistic montages. This has led to a somewhat standardized portrayal of landscape when it comes to "views". What remains so appealing about manual drawing is that the sensibility of the designer is embedded in the marking, like a signature, and so the line work is more immediately qualitative. The drawing conveys a sentiment or mood, more than just a likeness. This should be equally true of digital work, and is something we need to strive for when using programs such as Photoshop. Images should be geared to convey design intent, rather than be "realistic".

Topography and surface

Relatedly, hardware and software are design tools to be used in the production of a project, not simply its representation. I push students to use digital techniques for project creation and exploration, and put a strong emphasis on output in the form of physical models. There is a craft to digital work, though it is not often thought about that way. This is especially true when virtual space drawings are built for output into 3D via computer numerical control (CNC) machines. Given the direct link between design information and construction information afforded by these machines, precision in virtual space is implicated in the craft of the physical artifact.

The following were produced by students at the Department of Landscape Architecture, School of Design, University of Pennsylvania.

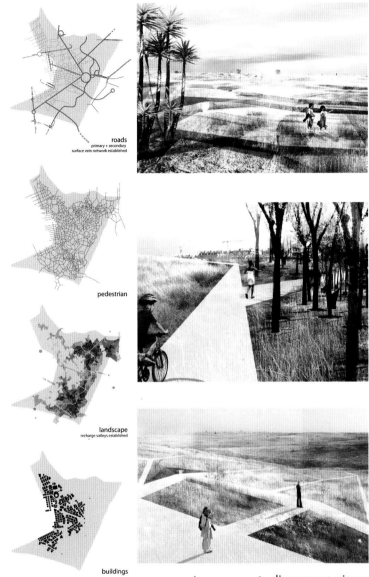

legacy scenario diagrams + views

23.1 a–n

Diagrams and collage perspectives for Olympics and post-Games legacy. Using the Olympic Games, the students studied the unique circumstances offered to landscape architecture by mega-events, in particular the demand for this particular site's rapid build-out over large tracts of land. Given the tension between fast-paced development and unknown future uses, as well as discrepancies in population-growth estimates, students were asked to consider how landscape could become both the image of the Games and the structure for development, thus combining the "logo" and the "legacy". In these images, the student compellingly conveys the distinction between the landscape during the Olympics and for its post-Games legacy. This is not a matter of using the same Photoshop image and simply removing people or increasing the size of the trees to show that time has passed. It conveys two different feelings. Notably, the images are not photorealistic. We have come to rely too much on "accurately" depicting a place rather than using images to convey imaginative, rather than literal, possibilities. By Tiffany Marston.

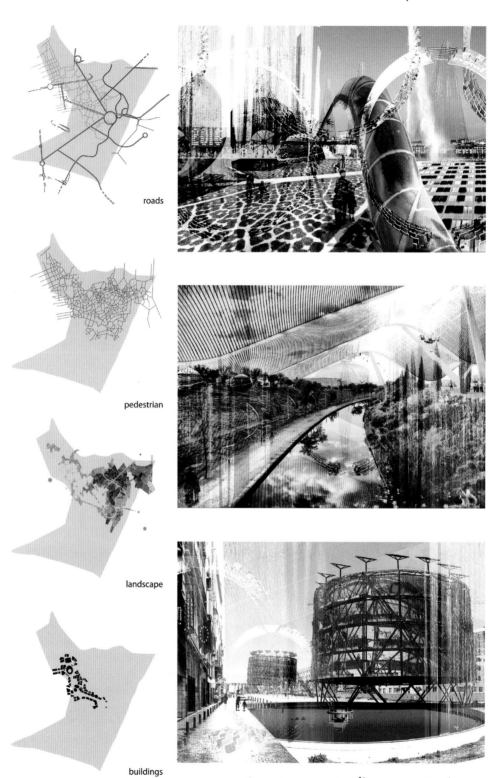

roads

pedestrian

landscape

buildings

olympic scenario diagrams + views

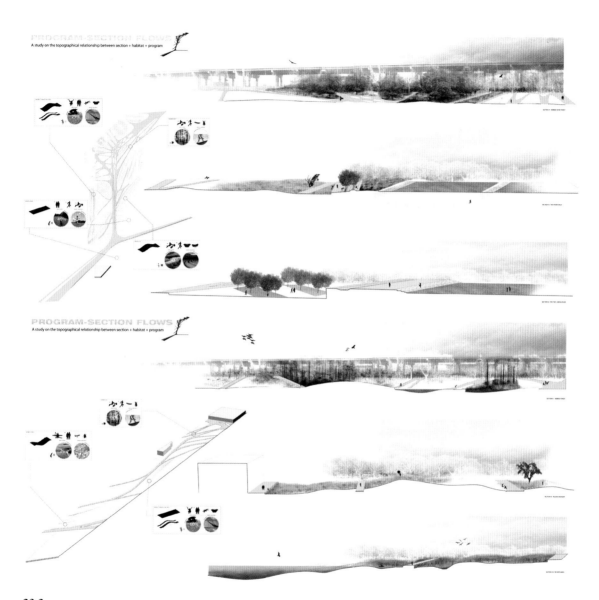

23.2
Diagrams and sections, section-perspectives for rural large field landscapes. Students in this first-year studio are asked to design a landscape for a 130-acre site with particular emphasis on constructing a variable ground plane. These drawings effectively highlight the relationship of circulation to topography and habitat. The yellow "splines" indicate the path system in both plan and section-perspective. The small diagrams keyed to the circulation plan indicate the percentage of habitat types, the associated topography, and the kinds of activities that it might support. This combination and relationship of drawings is more effective than a comprehensive plan in conveying the student's idea. By Alejandro Vazquez.

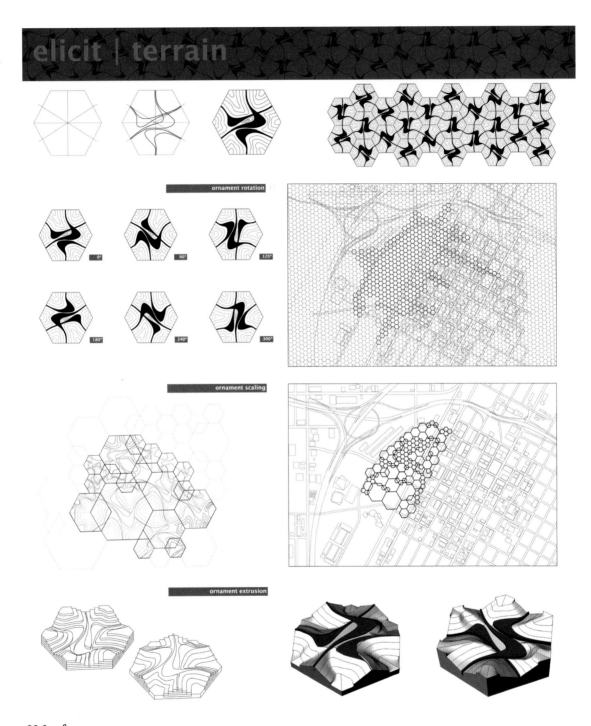

23.3 a–f
Digital model exploration (printed on panel) – development of initial closed modular unit based on a hexagon, and two options for possible site. By Francisco Allard.

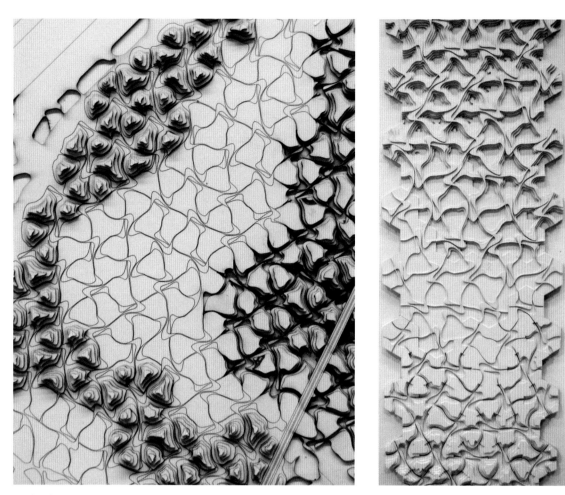

23.4 a–b
Digitally fabricated model CNC images show two options for how the module might be transformed by manipulating the interior of its topography – these models show the method of aggregating a unit (drawing) and the variable topography that can result (study models). The use of Rhinoceros software and laser-cutter technology enables the precise study of the topography. This studio had a specific methodology that emphasized the creation of topography through techniques of ornamentation, namely modularity and repetition. Initially, a series of exercises were undertaken so students could learn the methodology for achieving such organizations. They began with either a closed-shape module (symmetrical in its x–y axis, repeats through various operations but results in a limited number of configurations) or an open-shaped module (asymmetrical in its x–y axis, aggregates in unforeseen ways to produce an infinite number of configurations). A third dimension was introduced in the z axis of both types, thereby expanding the potential configurations when the units were aggregated. By Francisco Allard.

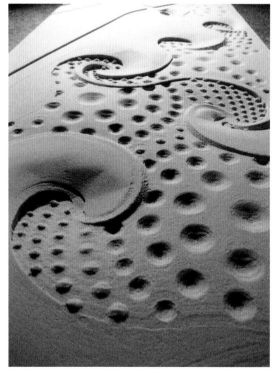

23.5 a

Digital perspective – bird's eye view. A field of solar "spikes" is layered onto two other organizations, creating a spectacle of light at night. The solar field and arabesque are boldly ornamental, in keeping with Las Vegas; they operate as framing mechanisms for a more delicate interior environment comprised of diverse habitats. This image is an aerial view of the site, clearly showing its context and conveying the mood of the landscape. By Joe Kubik.

23.5 b

Digitally fabricated model. This project utilized structural principles derived from desert plants to craft the site's surface. This happens at two scales: the overall topography and circulation is an arabesque form that frames an interior. The interior is a topography made of mounds and depressions that are distributed in a gradient that juxtaposes extremes of wet/dry, dormant/active, high/low, concave/convex. This project utilizes Rhinoceros for modeling and the model is fabricated using the CNC mill. By Joe Kubik.

23.5 c
Digital perspective – eye view. This image provides a contrasting view by locating the viewer within the landscape. By Joe Kubik.

24 Landscape Visualization

Rachel Berney

At the University of Southern California (USC), we encourage our students to fully explore the international laboratory that is LA – a multi-cultural region in an extraordinary natural landscape with complex ecological relationships. Los Angeles opens the extremes and the in-betweens of urban conditions and of landscape architecture possibilities. Thus the study of landscape architecture at USC has a particular focus on urban place-making in relation to three principles:

- First, our emphasis is on truly advanced study, based on the knowledge and skills to engage complex issues and to undertake ambitious explorations.
- Second, our emphasis is on urban landscapes, and on the responsibility of design professions to create the qualities and meanings of our urban futures.
- Third, we believe that place-making is fundamentally a collaborative responsibility that requires leadership from professionals across the entire domain of planning and design.

These images from the Landscape Architecture Program at the University of Southern California represent a range of design inquiry, analysis and synthesis. From mid-review studio models in cardboard to final rendered perspectives, students are pushed to critically explore places through visual and spatial analysis, as well as depict their analyses and design synthesis in dynamic visual form.

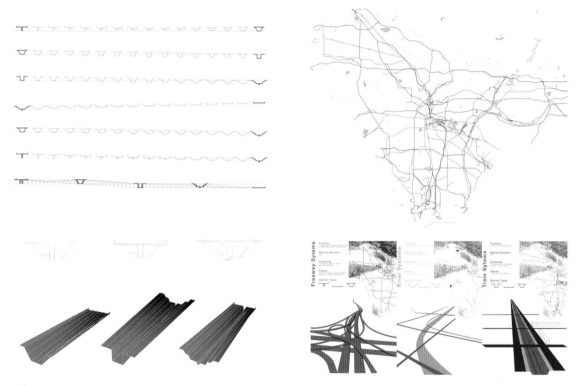

24.1
LA infrastructure – diagrams, perspectives and catalog. AutoCAD, Adobe Illustrator, Adobe Photoshop, Rhino, V-Ray.
Focused on LA's "Not a Cornfield" 32-acre site, the student analyzes the space as part of a systematic inventory of natural
and cultural events that create the site's configuration, history and sense of place within the city landscape. This site will
become a new urban park for downtown LA. The student analyzes and depicts his understanding of how this space has
been shaped over time and how it will serve the city in the future. By Gary Garcia.

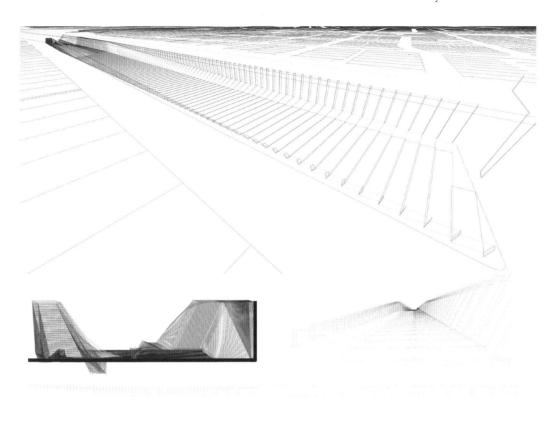

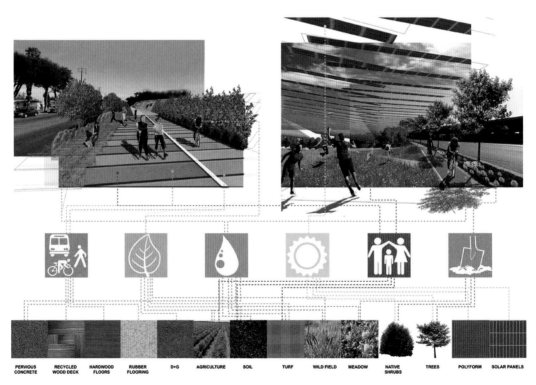

PERVIOUS CONCRETE   RECYCLED WOOD DECK   HARDWOOD FLOORS   RUBBER FLOORING   D+G   AGRICULTURE   SOIL   TURF   WILD FIELD   MEADOW   NATIVE SHRUBS   TREES   POLYFORM   SOLAR PANELS

24.2–24.3
Topographic Infrastructure: Hollywood Freeway Central Park, digital model (24.2); view from vehicle (24.3), using Rhino, Adobe Photoshop and Adobe Illustrator. In this award-winning project, the student explores how a park that caps a freeway could, along the upper surface, reconnect the communities divided by the Hollywood Freeway (the 101) via lively, programmed green urban surface, and below the freeway itself create an interesting experience for drivers. By Meng Yang.

24.4

Field, cardboard model. Also exploring the "Not a Cornfield" site in another studio, this work is part of the mapping, documentation and synthesis – urban research – used to explore the site. The "Not a Cornfield" site is one of many under-utilized spaces in the city that is being re-imagined, incorporating it into the city's fabric and using it to help support the 10,000 people who will move into the LA Metro area each year over the next thirty years. The student depicts his understanding of the site at mid-review through a model that uses cardboard, paper and glue. By Gabe Mason.

PATHS OF MOVEMENT roadways and trails   CONFLICTING BOUNDARIES across political thresholds   PARKLAND MOSAIC public vs. private realm   DEFINED PERMEABILITY scenic overlooks   VALUABLE ENVIRONMENT significant ecological areas

24.5 a–e

Reclaiming Mulholland. Adobe Illustrator, Adobe Photoshop. This analysis of the Mulholland Drive corridor is set within a study that counters the notion of LA as decentralized megalopolis and considers the LA basin as the ultimate urban–wild land interface, contained within the confines of the Pacific Ocean, Santa Monica Mountains and San Gabriel Mountains. Mulholland Drive is an east–west route through this basin that touches upon sensitive ecological zones, estates of the rich and famous, and famous movie locations. Upon careful analysis, the Mulholland corridor can be seen as a linear site with challenging contrasts between what is built and what is natural. This design project claims Mulholland as a space for people, a network of public parks for both everyday use and sublime experiences of built/natural interaction. By Larkin Owens.

25 systems | site | program | place

Jason Sowell

The means by which landscapes are represented influences how they are interpreted. As abstractions, or even idealizations, the types of representation models utilized in the design process privilege, if not prejudice, how one describes the cultural and natural systems of which the landscape is composed.[1] By extension, different representation models each delineate the "real" or "designed" landscape in distinct ways, whereby diagram, detail or perspectival projection juxtapose scales of site and program as a means of rendering phenomena and experience.

Current representation practices and pedagogy build upon landscape's historical utilization of measure and overlay, survey and transect, spreadsheet and database to index soils, vegetation, hydrology, or even demographics. Additionally, the adaptation of methods indigenous to cartography, anthropology, art and architecture (such as collage, superposition, scaling or folding) further figures phenomena and information as not only subjects of design, but the underlying parameters that engender a project's poetic and spatial dynamic.[2] In essence, the process positions representation as a dialectic for defining and designing the landscape. The drawing or model thereby transcends from mere image to an evaluative tool, such that representation unfolds as a set of operations that reference or register gaps and overlaps between existing systems and networks. In so doing, these operations delineate sites within these systems, such that program evolves as a narrative by which formal and structural relationships are established.

Teaching representation thereby reinforces an ability to assess and assimilate, in as much as utilize, a set of tools and techniques. The conceptual framework for understanding what to draw remains as critical as how to draw, as evidenced by the landscape discipline's reliance on research and data collection as a generative process through which information and circumstance are constructed and encoded. As projects have increased in complexity, the contextualization of a project's limits within a larger set of cultural and natural systems has led to the need, through representation, to define sites and invent programs. The subsequent harvesting of data required to formulate these sites and programs, as well as the manner in which the data's spatial implications are evaluated and mapped, have established a design process by which material and experiential decisions emerge from efforts to increasingly delineate the landscape's ecological, economic and social foundations.

As Dalibor Vesely notes, drawings, models, projective techniques and simulations provide the design process with the means by which conceptual intent "relates to the concrete situations of the everyday."[3] The artifacts that result from this endeavor remain fundamental to how designers visualize spatial relationships, construct a coherent argument, and communicate how the resulting sequence establishes place and experience. As representation models proceed from description to assessment, formulation to intervention, it is important that a modeling framework inform how one derives, anticipates and articulates intended spatial effects. Towards these ends, both functional analysis and programmatic speculation stage the landscape's transformation over time.

The following figures were produced by students in the Department of Landscape Architecture, University of Texas at Austin.

Notes

1   Representation models, as defined here, include two-dimensional and three-dimensional drawings, physical or digital models and databases.
2   The literature describing the conceptual and theoretical foundations underlying this view of representation is extensive. See, among others, Denis Cosgrove's "Mapping meaning" and James Corner's "The agency of mapping: speculation, critique, and invention," in Cosgrove's edited collection *Mappings* (London: Reaktion Books, 1999); de Sola-Morales, M., "The culture of description," *Perspecta*, 25, 1989, pp. 16–25; Corner, J. "Eidetic operations and new landscapes," in *Recovering Landscape* (New York: Princeton Architectural Press, 1999), pp. 153–70; Steele, B. "Design as research," *Daidalos*, 69/70, 1998/99, 54–59; Somol, R.E. "Dummy text, or the diagrammatic basis of contemporary architecture," in Peter Eisenman, ed., *Diagram Diaries* (New York: Rizzoli, 1999), pp. 6–25.
3   Vesely, D. *Architecture in the Age of Divided Representation: The Question of Creativity in the Shadow of Production*. Cambridge, MA: MIT Press, 2004.

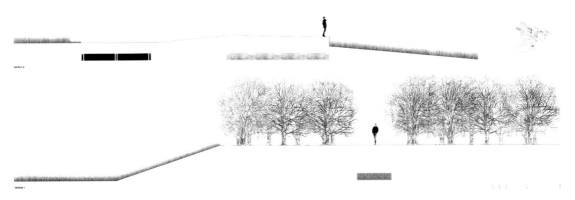

25.1 a–b
Sections, graphite, photocopy transfer, self-adhesive film on Stonehenge paper. Partial site sections depicting topographic manipulation, soil layers, vegetation change. Plant texture's influence on spatial volume is emphasized. By Noah Halbach.

25.2 a–d
Plan/map, graphite, photocopy transfer, self-adhesive film on Stonehenge paper. Analytical mapping of seasonal water fluctuations and its impact on bird habitat. A larger composite map of regional fluvial shifts, surface water levels and flood heights is juxtaposed with diagrams that depict which zones provide habitat for specific bird species during the spring, summer and fall seasons. By Yvonne Ellis.

25.3 a–b
Perspective, graphite and "verithin" pencil on white trace overlaid onto digital site photographs. In order to test and develop the project primarily in perspective, successive layers of graphite on trace are successively drawn, scanned, plotted and redrawn. By Brooks Rosenberg.

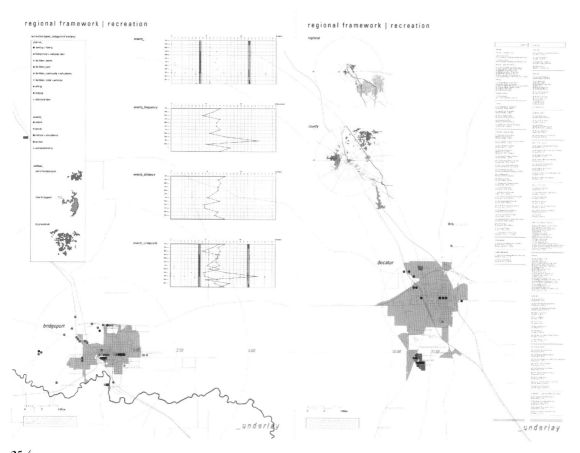

25.4

Mapping diagrams, raster and vector-based images. Partial programmatic diagram. Specific program and infrastructural proposals are documented, including calculations for area occupied, projected costs, and anticipated economic and ecological impact. By Sandi Veras.

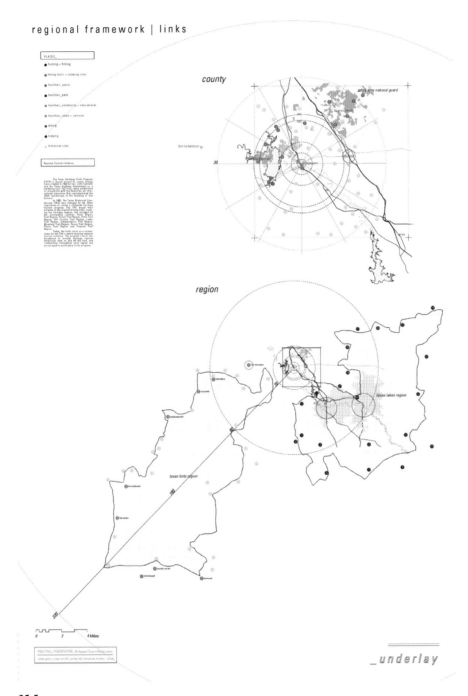

25.5

Mapping diagrams, raster and vector-based images. Phasing diagram and resource mapping.
Compiled from various agency and engineering reports, the mapping locates and demonstrates
proposed programs at the State and San Joaquin Valley scales. By Sandi Veras.

26 Drawing Objectives from the Landscape

Michelle Arab

Many of us are drawn to landscape architecture because of its ephemeral qualities, but how to represent those qualities graphically can be a challenge. Through hand-drawing, collage and mixed media with charcoal as the unifying materials, my students (at the University of Washington, College of Built Environment, Department of Landscape Architecture) explored how to depict the poetry of landscape through different types of assignments, including defining the essence of a word, mapping a campus square, and expressing the qualities of a project site.

Rather than focusing on spatial elements or data-driven information, the drawings captured the more intangible qualities of a site, such as its sounds, temperature, moisture and light, that can change over the course of a day, as well as through the seasons. Though still charged with the need to be informative and created with rigor, these drawings visualized qualities such as the sound of rain on different kinds of surfaces, the blurring of edges in twilight, and the smell of the sea in the city.

Understanding the qualities of a site is an important part in the design process. The students' observations and methods of notation revealed unexpected aspects of a place that influenced their comprehension of that place and their subsequent designs. Beyond simply analyzing a site, their investigations focused on the notion of creating new opportunities (or worlds).

Using only graphite pencil and/or charcoal, and sometimes materials taken from the site, the students were forced to abandon certain conventions that color allows. For example, water could not be represented with blue. Instead, the students determined alternative methods to describe water and its qualities. While at first this limited palette felt frustrating, the students were forced to explore and play with unconventional techniques to manipulate the media to communicate their ideas.

26.1 a–e
Park sections.
Charcoal, ink, leaf
residue, water.
Technique used:
crumpling paper to
add depth in the
topography, creating
makeshift stamps
to suggest foliage,
and layering various
combinations of ink
and water to suggest
seeping. By Cami
Culbertson.

26.2 a–c
Site sections.
Charcoal, ink, leaf
residue, water.
Technique used:
crumpling paper to
add depth in the
topography, creating
makeshift stamps
to suggest foliage,
and layering various
combinations of ink
and water to suggest
seeping. By Cami
Culbertson.

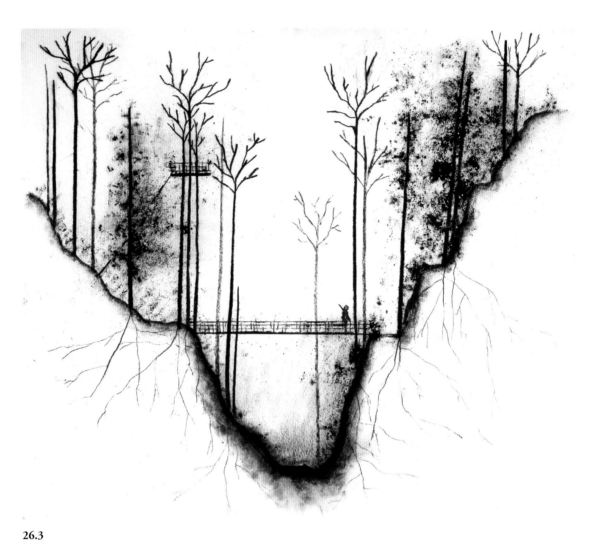

26.3
Ravine section. Using charcoal, the student draws a dark line to show the section cut, which gradually becomes heavier as the ravine becomes wetter and deeper. The student grinds the charcoal into the paper with a hammer to represent the evergreen plants. The tall, exaggerated trees and the roots show the verticality of the site and its depth. By Lindsey Gadbois.

26.4
Section. Charcoal, graphite, rubber cement and India ink. The student draws the base sketch using charcoal and then covers the charcoal with rubber cement. As it dries, the student uses an eraser to pull off rubber cement and charcoal. This technique creates texture for this particular landscape. The student pours India ink to represent water flow through the site and blows it across the page to create an organic, root-like form. By Matt Knorr.

26.5

Section. Charcoal, ink and soil on watercolor paper. The section is illustrated from the sound of the creek, the density of plants, and the differences in plants and elevation between the two sides that converge at the stream. Through recalling the experience on both sides of the creek, the student depicts each side's shade and depth of trees and shrubs, and the difference in varying elevation. By Win Leerasanthanah.

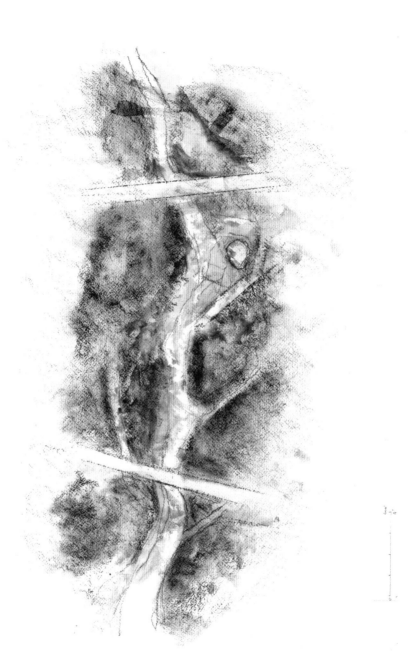

26.6

Plan. Charcoal and brush on watercolor paper. The student uses charcoal, ink and soil to capture the key aspects of the landscape. The charcoal medium determines the light and dark value and density of the forest as the dry brush media focuses on the wet and dry aspects of the site, particularly the sound of the creek that flows through the park. By Win Leerasanthanah.

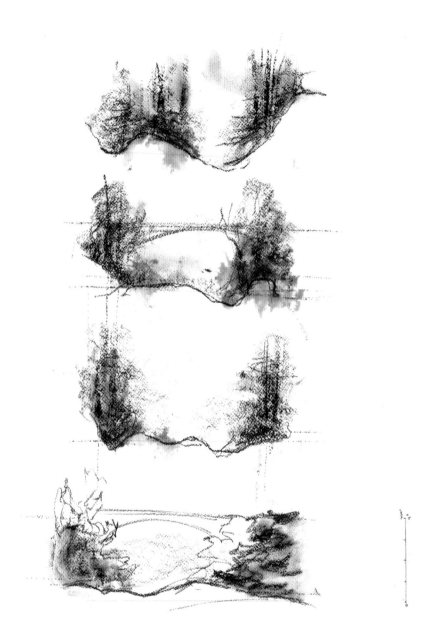

26.7 a–d
Series of sections. Charcoal and brush on watercolor paper. The illustration is done from a rough sketch of the section as the student walked through the park. The sections are later refined. By Win Leerasanthanah.

27 Modeling Landscapes

Jeffrey Hou

At a recent show at the Museum of Modern Art (MoMA) in New York, titled *Matisse: Radical Invention, 1913–17*, one finds Matisse's sculptural work displayed in juxtaposition with his early paintings. A series of work titled "Backs" seemingly resembles the figures in Matisse's signature paintings. Listening to the narrator in my audio tour, I learned that Matisse often studied his subject through sculpture prior to working in painting. He also went back and forth between the two modes of working. This hybrid approach forged a powerful interpretation of the human figure, an endlessly complex form whose representation has changed with minds and time.

The making of study models in design is not unlike the making of sculpture in Matisse's art. Model making has long been a highly effective method in design and representation. However, the recent discussion on landscape representation has focused predominantly on two-dimensional illustrations, with little discussion of model making as an equally relevant and important method. As such, the power of model making in the design process is often undervalued and poorly understood.

The selected models here highlight the instrumentality of model making as a pedagogical tool in landscape representation and design. Specifically, they demonstrate the narrative power of three-dimensional objects, the tactility of model making as a medium, and the tacit dialog between hands and mind, viewer and objects, a mode of representation that invites repeated observation and reinterpretation. Rough study models are often a quick and easy way to help communicate concepts in the spatial sense.

In a project titled "Biographical Landscapes" (27.1), the student used found objects to create a three-dimensional collage of landscapes that embody and represent the life experiences of three generations of their families or people they live with. The model helped connect the student's personal experiences and encounters to an understanding of landscape process and the making of the built environment. Through this modeling exercise, an exploration of the dynamic nature of landscape in the context of broader social, economic and political transformation in society was achieved, as well as explorations of representation of landscape narratives through three-dimensional collage. Sketch models provide opportunities for examining the effectiveness of different techniques and strategies for representation. The use of found objects, in particular, engages students in deliberate acts of appropriation and reinterpretation. As a beginning design exercise, the outcomes of this assignment provide a foundation in which social issues, environmental processes and design practice can be reconnected and re-examined.

The models in 27.2–27.4 are from a project titled "Union Bay Waterfront 10/20/50", in a first-year studio focusing on landform and ecological processes. The central idea of this studio is that designed landscapes can perform ecological functions through a wide variety of formal geometries instead of naturalistic forms. In the final studio project, students are asked to develop their design for stormwater retention and filtration on a waterfront site using a simple working model (scale: 1" = 50'). They also work simultaneously through mapping and time-series diagrams to represent habitat relationships and changes over time through processes such as deposition and erosion. Using a common palette of modeling clay for landform, wooden sticks (various sizes and thickness) for vegetation, and other optional materials, students were asked to develop and repeatedly rework a design that incorporates specific strategies for: (1) improving the quality of water released from the site; (2) enhancing the suitability of the site for a specific species to live, forage and/or reproduce; and (3) revealing the ecological dynamics of the site to human visitors over the next twenty years. Using models, students worked to represent how dynamic processes interact with landform.

Landscape model making provides a hands-on and iterative approach for students to develop and visually represent the dynamic interactions between form and processes. Specifically, model making using found objects and tactical associations provides an effective pedagogical tool for examining the representation of landscape meanings and narratives. As part of the learning process in beginning design in particular, model making is critical for students to develop a tactile understanding of space, forms and processes, an important foundation for a rigorous and more nuanced exploration of landscape representation and design.

27.1

This model depicts a garden as the physical and symbolic space of connection between different generations of a family. Instead of illustrating the individual gardens, we see elements representing traces and reminders from each generation contained within a single frame that can be pulled apart. The model impels us to wander through a collection of objects to reconstruct memories and connections. It underscores the complexity of movement, struggles, conflicts and affinity between the generations. By Lisa Reynolds.

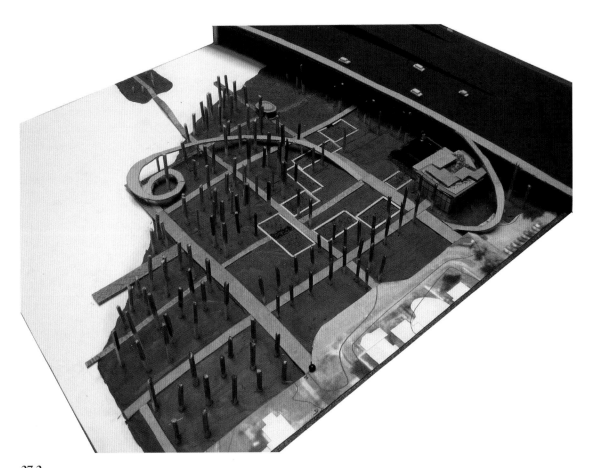

27.2
This project utilizes the geometry of the street grid to articulate the location of the site between a freshwater shoreline, a residential neighborhood and a state highway, and to serve as circulation throughout the site. The gridded pattern is interrupted by a series of cascading stormwater detention ponds that capture runoff from the highway, as well as an elevated walkway suspended above the water's edge. The wooden sticks painted in different colors represent different species of vegetation. By Justin Martin.

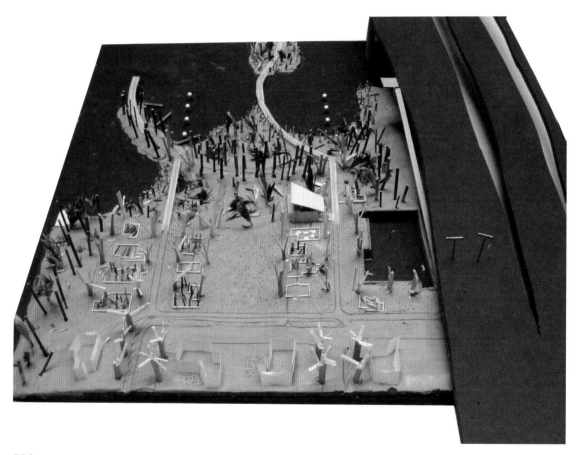

27.3

This project uses footprints of buildings as modules to organize different design features on site – a large detention pond next to the highway, and a series of gardens that line with the houses next to the site. Two arms extending into the bay provide both human access to the water and a barrier to protect the shallow-water habitats. They also provide the visual frame that mediates between land and water. By Matthew Martenson.

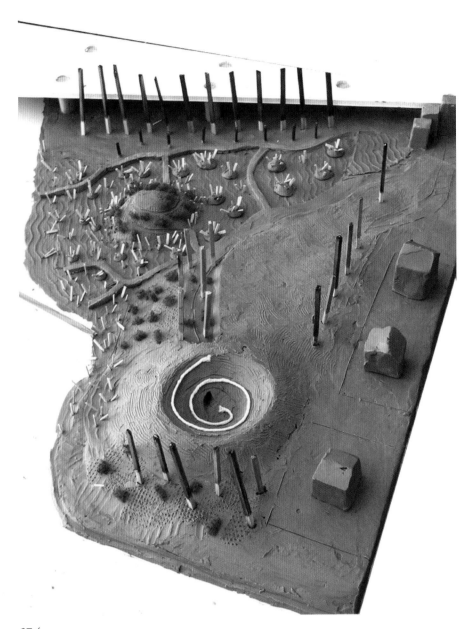

27.4

The two main features of the site design, a depression and a mound, serve two primary functions of the site – a stormwater facility and a place for experience. The depression is occupied by terracing wetland/ponds with a small mound in the middle to serve as a habitat for birds; the large mound further from the highway provides a vista for visitors. The contrasting form between the two establishes a dichotomy and a dialog between visitors and environmental processes. By David Minnery.

28 The Visual Message
Final thoughts

Nadia Amoroso

Visualizing the landscape is not only an art, but requires one to think critically and imaginatively about the means and method of conveying a specific visual message. The choice of style plays a large role in determining the landscape character that will engage the audience and showcase the concept and mood of the landscape. Introductory visual communication, visual representation and graphics courses for landscape architecture provide students with the opportunity to develop and test various modes of drawing using a palette of methods, styles and media, while building upon a lexis of design communication. Graphics courses give students the chance to see the important relationship between observing, conceptualizing, constructing and visually communicating an image or idea. The toolkit of drawing conventions is vast, and includes plans, sections, elevations, figure ground drawings, collage, perspectives, diagramming and mapping, and hybrid drawings composed manually and digitally. Students often tend to craft a branding of their visual work over the course of their studies, pushing the boundaries of contemporary design communication. Representing the landscape thoughtfully requires an imaginative, creative and rigorous approach. But how does one articulate the relationship between design ideas and their effective representation? It's been my experience that experimentation with various landscape types, moods, atmospheres, characters and spatial quality in visual depictions allows students to develop a broader range of artful skills. Encouraging students to try a variety of media, styles and modes of representation is crucial, as it enables them to test the multiple potentials of representation. Finally, building upon students' drawing and digital skills, individual strengths and diversity in design representation helps them to develop their own personal "brand", effectively giving them direction and purpose in their work.

A series of various landscape drawings composed using various media and styles is profiled within *Representing Landscapes*. Industrial and residual landscapes are characterized visually using charcoal and soft graphite on large, good-quality paper that is slightly textured. Profiled residual and relic landscapes include industrial sites, abandoned landscape, prairie fields, railway corridors, hydro- and petroleum stations, and farmland areas (28.1–28.6). The various techniques and styles used with this medium express the individual poetic beauty of the chosen landscapes. Main structural outlines of the image can be lightly drawn using an H or HB charcoal pencil on paper. Once the main structural outlines of the drawing are completed, the scene can begin to be rendered in detail. The application of key shades and shadows to the drawing adds visual depth to the space, and an eraser can be used to highlight specific areas of image and to lighten spaces. Other elements and landscape features are later collaged into these traditionally composed drawings. Creative Photoshopping – including advanced filtering, atmospheric changes, hue enhancement and other image mediation – transforms traditionally drawn images into expressive hybrid drawings that harmoniously fuse the digital and traditional (28.7–28.12).

Collage–montage is now the standard medium and visual representation type in the field of landscape architecture. Students are composing eye-catching perspectives, plans and sections quickly and effectively. Using Photoshop, they build upon simple rough-sketch perspective drawings and transform them into captivating spaces that demonstrate the possibilities of interior and exterior environments. Textures and other "digitally cut" elements scanned from magazines or journals, or extracted from the web or other visual sources, are layered to craft new situations. Elements in the foreground should be more distinguishable than the background elements, which provide visual depth to the scene when lower levels of opacity are used. Stretching and blurring background textures can help to fill the areas and emphasize the perspective when necessary. Applying a slight blur onto people or vehicles in the angle of the motion direction provides a sense of movement to these elements in the constructed perspectives. Adding people engaged in activity or in positions relating to the landscape, such as joggers along a waterfront boardwalk or people sitting on a grassy field watching a baseball game, enhances the quality of the landscape being represented. Applying a level of transparency onto people may evoke a sense of temporality, suggesting that the users are occupying that same landscape for a brief moment. Experimenting with levels of occupancy, blurring and other filters is encouraged. The key is to avoid over-Photoshopping with unnecessary filters and other superfluous elements. Keeping the representation simple, creative and eye-catching helps to engage visually with the audience (28.13–28.19).

The following visual catalog, by students at the University of Toronto, demonstrates how landscape character and proposed designs can be successfully expressed through traditional drawing, digital image modification, or a hybrid of the two.

28.1–28.6

Charcoal drawings on large-textured, good quality paper, depicting scenes including farmland, post-industrial urban center, hydro-line corridor, landscape, open fields. 28.6 is composed using soft and dark tones of graphite to depict highway infrastructure. By Karen May (28.1), Peggy Pei-Chi Chi (28.2), Han Liu (28.3), Justin Miron (28.4), Jessie Gresley-Jones (28.5) and Stephanie Cheng (28.6).

28.7–28.12

These collage perspective are depictions developed from their respective charcoal/graphite drawings, comparing the two styles and media representing the same landscape types. The base charcoal/graphite drawing is either scanned or photographed and later brought into Photoshop as a based layer. Elements and textures are superimposed and added to the based images, altering the feel and overall final landscape representation. Filters and color adjustment, and lighting filters, are applied to the overall images. By Karen May (28.7), Peggy Pei-Chi Chi (28.8), Han Liu (28.9), Justin Miron (28.10), Jessie Gresley-Jones (28.11) and Stephanie Cheng (28.12).

28.13–28.14
Collage perspective with digital model base composed using 3ds Max, superimposed onto campus photographic background. 28.13 depicts a night scene composed with dark layer wash with light transparency. White featured shapes draw lighting features to the attention of the reader. 28.14 depicts same landscape campus in a winter scene. Transparent silhouette figures add scale to the drawing while presenting a clean and simple rendering of users of the space. White speckled brush strokes overlaid on the drawing add snow flakes to the ultimate winter scene. By Ana Espinosa.

28.15–28.16
Night rendering scenes. 28.15 applies lighting
shaped by a marquee outline in Photoshop followed
by white-yellow transparent overlay onto dark scene.
By Liu Xin. 28.16 depicts a striking aerial view
of a designed urban square with media board and
lighting effects to depict a night scene. By Jeffrey
Cock.

28.17–28.18
Poetically rendered collage perspectives developed onto a based digital massing form composed in Rhinoceros software. The digital model is imported as raster image base-tiff or jpg, and elements and textures are applied for scene development followed by various opacity levels. Elements in the background have a lower opacity level, while features in the foreground are less transparent. By Shadi Edarehchi Gilani (28.17) and Zahra Awang (28.18).

1:250   10m

Justin Miron
Yorkville Park Plan-Elevation

28.19
Collage section with elements of the plan and material placed directly below the cut-line, presenting a relationship
between plan, section and material in one drawing. By Justin Miron.

Index